Simple 1-2-3™
Chicken

Publications International, Ltd.
Favorite Brand Name Recipes at www.fbnr.com

Microwave Cooking: Microwave ovens vary in wattage. Use the cooking times as guidelines and check for doneness before adding more time.

Preparation/Cooking Times: Preparation times are based on the approximate amount of time required to assemble the recipe before cooking, baking, chilling or serving. These times include preparation steps such as measuring, chopping and mixing. The fact that some preparations and cooking can be done simultaneously is taken into account. Preparation of optional ingredients and serving suggestions is not included.

Contents

Easy Appetizers

Garlicky Gilroy Chicken Wings

2 pounds chicken wings
(about 15 wings)
2 heads fresh garlic,
separated into cloves
and peeled*
1 cup olive oil plus
additional for greasing
1 teaspoon hot pepper
sauce, or to taste
1 cup grated Parmesan
cheese
1 cup Italian-style bread
crumbs
1 teaspoon black pepper
Carrot and celery slices
for garnish

To peel whole heads of garlic, drop garlic heads into enough boiling water in small saucepan to cover for 5 to 10 seconds. Immediately remove garlic with slotted spoon. Plunge garlic into cold water; drain. Peel away skins.

1. Preheat oven to 375°F.

2. For each wing, cut through first and second joints using sharp knife on cutting board; remove and discard tips. Rinse wings and pat dry with paper towels.

3. Place garlic, 1 cup oil and hot pepper sauce in food processor; cover and process until smooth. Pour garlic mixture into small bowl. Combine cheese, bread crumbs and black pepper in shallow dish. Dip wings, one at a time, into garlic mixture, then roll in crumb mixture, coating evenly and shaking off excess.

4. Grease 13×9-inch nonstick baking pan; arrange wings in single layer in pan. Drizzle remaining garlic mixture over wings; sprinkle with remaining crumb mixture. Bake 45 to 60 minutes or until wings are brown and crisp. Garnish, if desired.

Makes about 6 servings

Chicken Tortilla Roll-Ups

4 ounces light cream
cheese, softened
2 tablespoons mayonnaise
1 tablespoon Dijon
mustard
¼ teaspoon black pepper
3 (10- to 12-inch) flour
tortillas
1 cup finely chopped
cooked chicken
¾ cup shredded or finely
chopped carrot
¾ cup finely chopped green
bell pepper
3 tablespoons chopped
green onion

1. Combine cream cheese, mayonnaise, mustard and black pepper in small bowl; stir until well blended.

2. Spread cream cheese mixture evenly onto each tortilla leaving ½-inch border. Sprinkle chicken, carrot, bell pepper and onion evenly over cream cheese leaving 1½-inch border on cream cheese mixture at one end of each tortilla.

3. Roll up each tortilla jelly-roll fashion. Cut each roll into 1½-inch-thick slices.   *Makes 5 to 6 appetizer servings*

Cook's Nook: Wrap rolls in plastic wrap and refrigerate for several hours for easier slicing and to allow flavors to blend.

Easy Appetizers

Spicy Chicken Bundles

1. Combine chicken, ginger, garlic and red pepper flakes in medium bowl.

2. Blend soy sauce into cornstarch in cup until smooth.

3. Heat wok or large skillet over medium-high heat. Add oil; heat until hot. Add chicken mixture; stir-fry 2 to 3 minutes until chicken is no longer pink.

4. Stir soy sauce mixture and add to wok. Stir-fry 30 seconds or until sauce boils and thickens. Add water chestnuts, onions and peanuts; heat through.*

5. Divide filling evenly among lettuce leaves; roll up. Secure with toothpicks. Serve warm or at room temperature. Do not let filling stand at room temperature more than 2 hours. Serve with hot mustard, if desired.

Makes 12 appetizers

Filling may be made ahead to this point; cover and refrigerate up to 4 hours. Just before rolling in lettuce, reheat chicken filling until warm. Proceed as directed in step 5.

Tip: Slice additional green onions into long strips and use to tie leaves in place around bundles.

1 pound ground chicken or turkey
2 teaspoons minced fresh ginger
2 cloves garlic, minced
¼ teaspoon red pepper flakes
3 tablespoons soy sauce
1 tablespoon cornstarch
1 tablespoon peanut or vegetable oil
⅓ cup finely chopped water chestnuts
⅓ cup thinly sliced green onions
¼ cup chopped peanuts
12 large lettuce leaves, such as romaine
Chinese hot mustard (optional)

Honey-Sauced Chicken Wings

3 pounds chicken wings
1 teaspoon salt
½ teaspoon black pepper
1 cup honey
½ cup soy sauce
¼ cup chopped onions
¼ cup ketchup
2 tablespoons vegetable oil
2 cloves garlic, minced
¼ teaspoon red pepper flakes
Toasted sesame seeds (optional)

Slow Cooker Directions

1. Preheat broiler. Rinse chicken and pat dry. Cut off and discard wing tips. Cut each wing at joint to make two sections. Sprinkle wing parts with salt and pepper. Place wings on broiler pan. Broil 4 to 5 inches from heat 20 minutes, 10 minutes a side or until chicken is brown. Place chicken into slow cooker.

2. For sauce, combine honey, soy sauce, onions, ketchup, oil, garlic and pepper flakes in bowl. Pour over chicken wings.

3. Cover; cook on LOW 4 to 5 hours or on HIGH 2 to 2½ hours. Garnish with sesame seeds, if desired. *Makes about 32 appetizers*

Easy Appetizers

Grilled Chicken Tostados

1. Place chicken in single layer in shallow glass dish; sprinkle with cumin. Combine orange juice, ¼ cup salsa, 1 tablespoon oil and garlic in small bowl; pour over chicken. Cover; marinate in refrigerator at least 2 hours or up to 8 hours, stirring mixture occasionally.

2. Prepare grill for direct cooking.

3. Drain chicken; reserve marinade. Brush green onions with remaining 2 teaspoons oil. Place chicken and green onions on grid. Grill, covered, over medium-high heat 5 minutes. Brush tops of chicken with half of reserved marinade; turn and brush with remaining marinade. Turn onions. Continue to grill, covered, 5 minutes or until chicken is no longer pink in center and onions are tender. (If onions are browning too quickly, remove before chicken is done.)

4. Meanwhile, combine beans and remaining 2 tablespoons salsa in small saucepan; cook, stirring occasionally, over medium heat until hot.

5. Place tortillas in single layer on grid. Grill, uncovered, 1 to 2 minutes per side or until golden brown. (If tortillas puff up, pierce with tip of knife or flatten by pressing with spatula.)

6. Transfer chicken and onions to cutting board. Slice chicken crosswise into ½-inch strips. Cut onions crosswise into 1-inch-long pieces. Spread tortillas with bean mixture; top with lettuce, chicken, onions, cheese, avocado and tomato, if desired. Sprinkle with cilantro and serve with sour cream, if desired.

Makes 8 servings

1 pound boneless skinless chicken breasts
1 teaspoon ground cumin
¼ cup orange juice
¼ cup plus 2 tablespoons salsa, divided
1 tablespoon plus 2 teaspoons vegetable oil, divided
2 cloves garlic, minced
8 green onions
1 can (16 ounces) refried beans
8 (6- to 7-inch) flour tortillas
2 cups chopped romaine lettuce
1½ cups (6 ounces) shredded Monterey Jack cheese with jalapeño peppers
1 ripe medium avocado, diced (optional)
1 medium tomato, seeded and diced (optional)
Chopped fresh cilantro and sour cream (optional)

Easy Appetizers

Chicken Empanadas

1 box (15 ounces)
 refrigerated pie crusts
 (two 11-inch rounds)
4 ounces cream cheese
2 tablespoons chopped
 fresh cilantro
2 tablespoons salsa
½ teaspoon ground cumin
½ teaspoon salt
¼ teaspoon garlic powder
1 cup finely chopped
 cooked chicken
1 egg, beaten
 Additional salsa

1. Remove pie crust pouches from box; let stand at room temperature 15 to 20 minutes.

2. Heat cream cheese in small heavy saucepan over low heat; cook and stir until melted. Add cilantro, salsa, cumin, salt and garlic powder; stir until smooth. Stir in chicken; remove from heat.

3. Unfold pie crusts; remove plastic film. Roll out slightly on lightly floured surface. Cut crusts into 3-inch rounds using biscuit cutter. Reroll pie crust scraps and cut enough additional to equal 20 rounds.

4. Preheat oven to 425°F. Line two baking sheets with foil. Place about 2 teaspoons chicken mixture in center of each round. Brush edges lightly with water. Pull one side of dough over filling to form half circle; pinch edges to seal.

5. Place 10 to 12 empanadas onto each prepared baking sheet; brush lightly with egg. Bake 16 to 18 minutes or until lightly browned. Serve with salsa.

Makes 10 appetizer servings

Note: Empanadas can be prepared ahead of time and frozen. Simply wrap unbaked empanadas in plastic wrap and freeze. To bake, unwrap and follow above directions baking 18 to 20 minutes.

Pie Crusts

Ground Cumin

Easy Appetizers

Chicken Wraps

1. Preheat toaster oven to 350°F. Sprinkle five spice powder over chicken thighs. Place on toaster oven tray. Bake 20 minutes or until chicken is no longer pink in center. Remove and dice chicken.

2. Place chicken in bowl. Add scallion, bean sprouts, almonds, hoisin sauce, chili sauce and soy sauce. Stir gently but well. To serve, spoon ⅓ cup chicken mixture onto each lettuce leaf; roll or fold as desired.   *Makes 4 servings*

½ teaspoon five spice powder
½ pound boneless skinless chicken thighs
2 tablespoons minced scallion, green parts only
½ cup bean sprouts, rinsed well and drained
2 tablespoons sliced almonds
4 teaspoons hoisin sauce
½ tablespoon hot chili sauce with garlic*
2 tablespoons soy sauce
4 large leaves romaine or iceberg lettuce

Hot chili sauce with garlic is available in the Asian foods section of most supermarkets.

Easy Appetizers

Pita Pizzas

½ pound boneless skinless chicken breasts
Nonstick cooking spray
½ cup thinly sliced red bell pepper
½ cup thinly sliced mushrooms
½ cup thinly sliced red onion (about 1 small)
2 cloves garlic, minced
1 teaspoon dried basil
½ teaspoon dried oregano
1 cup torn fresh spinach leaves
6 mini whole wheat pita breads
½ cup (2 ounces) shredded part-skim mozzarella cheese

1. Preheat oven to 375°F. Cut chicken into ½-inch cubes. Spray medium nonstick skillet with cooking spray; heat over medium heat until hot. Add chicken; cook and stir 6 minutes or until browned and cooked through. Remove chicken from skillet.

2. Spray same nonstick skillet again with cooking spray; add bell pepper, mushrooms, onion, garlic, basil and oregano. Cook and stir over medium heat 5 to 7 minutes or until vegetables are crisp-tender. Return chicken to skillet; stir well.

3. Place spinach on top of pita breads. Divide chicken and vegetable mixture evenly; spoon over spinach. Sprinkle evenly with mozzarella cheese. Bake, uncovered, 7 to 10 minutes or until cheese is melted. *Makes 6 servings*

Easy Appetizers

Grilled Chicken Skewers

Spray grill grate with CRISCO® Cooking Spray; heat grill. Thread chicken on skewers; grill over medium heat, turning once, 10 to 12 minutes or until cooked through. Brush with 1 cup Southern Style Barbecue Sauce during last few minutes of cooking. Serve with remaining 1 cup sauce.

Makes 10 to 12 skewers

Prep Time: *15 minutes*
Cook Time: *1 hour, 10 to 12 minutes*

Southern-Style Barbecue Sauce

In a large saucepan, heat CRISCO® Oil over medium heat. Add celery, pepper and onion; sauté until soft. Add ketchup and sugar. Reduce heat to low; stir until sugar dissolves. Add remaining ingredients; cook on very low heat, stirring occasionally, for 1 hour.

Makes 2 cups

CRISCO® No-Stick
   Cooking Spray
1 pound chicken tenders
10 to 12 wooden skewers,
   soaked in water for
   30 minutes
   Southern-Style Barbecue
   Sauce (recipe follows)

⅓ cup CRISCO® Vegetable
   Oil*
1 stalk celery, finely
   chopped
½ *each* red and green bell
   pepper, finely chopped
1 small onion, finely
   chopped
2 cups ketchup
¾ cup dark brown sugar
¼ cup yellow mustard
2 tablespoons
   Worcestershire sauce
2 tablespoons lemon juice
1 tablespoon garlic powder
1 tablespoon ground ginger
¾ teaspoon salt
½ teaspoon black pepper
¼ teaspoon cayenne pepper
¼ teaspoon chili powder

Or use your favorite CRISCO® Oil

Easy Appetizers

Savory Chicken Satay

1 envelope LIPTON®
    RECIPE SECRETS®
    Onion Soup Mix
¼ cup BERTOLLI® Olive Oil
2 tablespoons firmly
    packed brown sugar
2 tablespoons SKIPPY®
    Peanut Butter
1 pound boneless, skinless
    chicken breasts,
    pounded and cut into
    thin strips
12 to 16 large wooden
    skewers, soaked in
    water

1. In large plastic bag, combine soup mix, oil, brown sugar and peanut butter. Add chicken and toss to coat well. Close bag and marinate in refrigerator 30 minutes.

2. Remove chicken from marinade, discarding marinade. On skewers, thread chicken, weaving back and forth.

3. Grill or broil skewers until chicken is thoroughly cooked. Serve with your favorite dipping sauces. *Makes 12 to 16 appetizers*

Prep Time: *15 minutes*
Marinate Time: *30 minutes*
Cook Time: *8 minutes*

Easy Appetizers

Bandito Buffalo Wings

PREHEAT oven to 375°F. Lightly grease 13×9-inch baking pan.

PLACE seasoning mix in heavy-duty plastic or paper bag. Add 3 chicken wings; shake well to coat. Place wings in prepared pan. Repeat until all wings have been coated.

BAKE for 35 to 40 minutes or until no longer pink near bone. Serve with salsa for dipping.

Makes 6 appetizer servings

1 package (1.25 ounces) ORTEGA® Taco Seasoning Mix
12 (about 1 pound *total*) chicken wings
ORTEGA Salsa (any flavor)

Chicken-Pesto Pizza

8 ounces chicken tenders
Nonstick cooking spray
1 medium onion, thinly
    sliced
⅓ cup prepared pesto
3 medium plum tomatoes,
    thinly sliced
1 (14-inch) prepared pizza
    crust
1 cup (4 ounces) shredded
    mozzarella cheese

1. Preheat oven to 450°F. Cut chicken tenders into bite-size pieces. Coat medium nonstick skillet with cooking spray; cook and stir chicken over medium heat 2 minutes. Add onion and pesto; cook and stir about 3 minutes or until chicken is cooked through.

2. Arrange tomato slices and chicken mixture on pizza crust to within 1 inch of edge. Sprinkle cheese over top. Bake 8 minutes or until pizza is hot and cheese is melted and bubbly.   *Makes 6 servings*

Prep and Cook Time: *22 minutes*

Easy Appetizers

Coconut Chicken Tenders with Spicy Mango Salsa

1. Combine mango, bell pepper, onion and cilantro in small bowl. Season to taste with salt and ground red pepper. Transfer half of mango salsa to food processor; process until finely chopped (almost puréed). Combine with remaining salsa. Set aside.

2. Preheat oven to 400°F. Spread coconut on large baking sheet. Bake 5 to 6 minutes or until lightly browned, stirring every 2 minutes. Transfer coconut to food processor; process until finely chopped but not pasty.

3. Beat egg with oil, salt and ground red pepper in small bowl. Add chicken tenders; toss to coat. Roll tenders in coconut; arrange on foil-lined baking sheet. Bake 18 to 20 minutes or until no longer pink in center. Serve with Spicy Mango Salsa. *Makes 5 to 6 servings*

1 firm ripe mango, peeled, seeded and chopped
½ cup chopped red bell pepper
3 tablespoons chopped green onion
2 tablespoons chopped fresh cilantro
1½ cups flaked coconut
1 egg
1 tablespoon vegetable oil
¼ teaspoon salt
Dash ground red pepper
¾ pound chicken tenders

Szechuan Chicken Tenders

2 tablespoons soy sauce
1 tablespoon chili sauce
1 tablespoon dry sherry
2 cloves garlic, minced
¼ teaspoon red pepper flakes
16 chicken tenders (about 1 pound)
1 tablespoon peanut oil
Hot cooked rice (optional)

1. Combine soy sauce, chili sauce, sherry, garlic and red pepper in shallow dish. Add chicken; coat well.

2. Heat oil in large nonstick skillet over medium heat until hot. Add chicken; cook 6 minutes, turning once, until chicken is browned and no longer pink in center.

3. Serve chicken with rice, if desired.   *Makes 4 servings*

Cook's Nook: If you can "take the heat," try adding a few Szechuan peppers to the dish. They are best if heated in the oven or over a low flame in a skillet for a few minutes beforehand.

Easy Appetizers

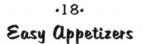

Apricot-Chicken Pot Stickers

1. Bring 2 cups water to a boil in medium saucepan. Add chicken. Reduce heat to low; simmer, covered, 10 minutes or until chicken is no longer pink in center. Remove from saucepan; drain.

2. Add cabbage and remaining 1 tablespoon water to saucepan. Cook over high heat 1 to 2 minutes or until water evaporates, stirring occasionally. Remove from heat; cool slightly.

3. Finely chop chicken. Add to saucepan along with preserves, green onions, soy sauce, ginger and pepper; mix well.

4. To assemble pot stickers, remove 3 wonton wrappers at a time from package. Spoon slightly rounded tablespoonful chicken mixture onto center of each wrapper; brush edges of wrapper with water. Bring 4 corners together; press to seal. Repeat with remaining wrappers and filling.

5. Spray steamer with nonstick cooking spray. Assemble steamer so that water is ½ inch below steamer basket. Fill steamer basket with pot stickers, leaving enough space between them to prevent sticking. Cover; steam 5 minutes. Transfer pot stickers to serving plate. Serve with prepared sweet-and-sour sauce, if desired.

Makes 10 servings

2 cups plus 1 tablespoon water, divided
2 boneless skinless chicken breasts (about 8 ounces)
2 cups chopped finely shredded cabbage
½ cup apricot preserves
2 green onions with tops, finely chopped
2 teaspoons reduced-sodium soy sauce
½ teaspoon grated fresh ginger
⅛ teaspoon black pepper
30 (3-inch) wonton wrappers
Prepared sweet-and-sour sauce (optional)

Simple Soups & Stews

Chicken Vegetable Soup

1 bag SUCCESS® Rice
5 cups chicken broth
1½ cups chopped uncooked chicken
1 cup sliced celery
1 cup sliced carrots
½ cup chopped onion
¼ cup chopped fresh parsley
½ teaspoon pepper
½ teaspoon dried thyme leaves, crushed
1 bay leaf
1 tablespoon lime juice

Prepare rice according to package directions.

Combine broth, chicken, celery, carrots, onion, parsley, pepper, thyme and bay leaf in large saucepan or Dutch oven. Bring to a boil over medium-high heat, stirring once or twice. Reduce heat to low; simmer 10 to 15 minutes or until chicken is no longer pink in center. Remove bay leaf; discard. Stir in rice and lime juice. *Makes 4 servings*

Chicken Tortilla Soup

2 large ripe avocados, halved and pitted
4 teaspoons TABASCO® brand Green Pepper Sauce, divided
½ teaspoon salt or to taste
3 (14½-ounce) cans chicken broth
3 boneless, skinless chicken breast halves (about 1 pound)
2 tablespoons uncooked rice
1 large tomato, seeded and chopped
½ cup chopped onion
¼ cup finely chopped cilantro
Tortilla chips
½ cup (2 ounces) shredded Monterey Jack cheese

Scoop out avocado into medium bowl and mash with fork. Add 1½ teaspoons TABASCO® Green Pepper Sauce and salt; blend gently but thoroughly. Set aside.

Heat chicken broth to boiling in 4-quart saucepan. Add chicken breast halves; reduce heat and cook until chicken is opaque. Remove chicken and cut into bite-size pieces. Add rice and cook about 15 minutes or until tender. Return chicken to saucepan. Just before serving, stir in tomato, onion, cilantro and remaining 2½ teaspoons TABASCO® Green Pepper Sauce.

To serve, break small handful of tortilla chips into bottom of each bowl. Ladle soup over tortilla chips. Top with cheese and 1 rounded tablespoon avocado mixture. Serve immediately with additional TABASCO® Green Pepper Sauce, if desired. *Makes 8 servings*

Black and White Chili

1. Spray large saucepan with cooking spray; heat over medium heat until hot. Add chicken and onion; cook and stir over medium to medium-high heat 5 to 8 minutes or until chicken is cooked through.

2. Stir beans, tomatoes with juice, and seasoning mix into saucepan; bring to a boil. Reduce heat to low; simmer, uncovered, 10 minutes.

Makes 6 servings

Serving Suggestion: For a change of pace, this delicious chili is excellent served over cooked rice or pasta.

Prep and Cook Time: *30 minutes*

Nonstick cooking spray

1 pound chicken tenders, cut into ¾-inch pieces

1 cup coarsely chopped onion

1 can (15½ ounces) Great Northern beans, rinsed and drained

1 can (15 ounces) black beans, rinsed and drained

1 can (14½ ounces) Mexican-style stewed tomatoes, undrained

2 tablespoons Texas-style chili powder seasoning mix

Potato Chicken Soup

2½ pounds DOLE® Red Potatoes, peeled, cut into 1-inch cubes
½ pound DOLE® Peeled Mini Carrots, halved
1 container (32 ounces) chicken broth
½ bay leaf
2 teaspoons olive oil
1 small onion, cut into 1-inch cubes
1 teaspoon dried tarragon leaves, crushed
¼ teaspoon dried thyme leaves, crushed
1½ cups cooked diced chicken
1 to 2 tablespoons minced parsley
⅛ teaspoon salt

• Combine potatoes, carrots, chicken broth and bay leaf in large pot. Bring to boil; reduce heat and simmer 15 to 20 minutes.

• Heat oil in nonstick skillet. Add onion; cook 6 to 8 minutes or until lightly browned. Add thyme and tarragon; cook 30 seconds.

• Add onion mixture, chicken, parsley and salt to soup in pot. Cook 5 minutes longer or until heated through. Remove bay leaf before serving.

Makes 4 servings

Prep Time: *25 minutes*
Cook Time: *35 minutes*

Confetti Chicken Chili

1. Heat large nonstick saucepan over medium heat until hot. Add chicken and onion; cook and stir 5 minutes or until chicken is browned. Drain fat from saucepan.

2. Add remaining ingredients to saucepan. Bring to a boil. Reduce heat to low and simmer 15 minutes. *Makes 5 servings*

Tip: To spice up this chunky chili, add 1 jalapeño pepper, finely chopped to saucepan with other ingredients.

Prep & Cook Time: *30 minutes*

1 pound ground chicken
1 large onion, chopped
2 cans (about 14 ounces each) fat-free reduced-sodium chicken broth
1 can (15 ounces) Great Northern beans, rinsed and drained
2 carrots, chopped
1 medium green bell pepper, chopped
2 plum tomatoes, chopped
2 teaspoons chili powder
½ teaspoon ground red pepper

Simple Soups & Stews

1 large fresh fennel bulb (about ¾ pound)
1 teaspoon olive oil
½ pound boneless skinless chicken thighs, cut into ¾-inch pieces
1 teaspoon dried rosemary, crushed
½ teaspoon black pepper
1 can (14½ ounces) no-salt-added stewed tomatoes
1 can (about 14 ounces) fat-free reduced-sodium chicken broth
1 can (15 ounces) cannellini beans, rinsed and drained
Hot pepper sauce (optional)

Tuscan Chicken with White Beans

1. Cut off and reserve ¼ cup chopped feathery fennel tops. Chop bulb into ½-inch pieces. Heat oil in large saucepan over medium heat. Add chopped fennel bulb; cook 5 minutes, stirring occasionally.

2. Sprinkle rosemary and pepper over chicken; add to saucepan. Cook and stir 2 minutes. Add tomatoes with juice and chicken broth; bring to a boil. Cover; simmer 10 minutes. Stir in beans; simmer, uncovered, 15 minutes or until chicken is cooked through and sauce thickens. Season to taste with hot pepper sauce, if desired. Ladle into 4 shallow bowls; top with reserved fennel tops.
Makes 4 servings

Prep Time: *15 minutes*
Cook Time: *35 minutes*

Sausage and Chicken Gumbo

1. Heat oil in large saucepan. Add bell pepper; cook and stir over medium-high heat 2 to 3 minutes. Add chicken; cook and stir about 2 minutes or until browned. Add sausage; cook and stir 2 minutes or until browned. Add broth; scrape up any browned bits from bottom of saucepan.

2. Add tomatoes, green onions, bay leaf, basil, black pepper and red pepper flakes. Simmer 15 minutes. Remove and discard bay leaf. Garnish each serving as desired.

Makes 6 servings

1 tablespoon canola oil
1 red bell pepper, chopped
1 pound boneless skinless chicken thighs, trimmed of excess fat and cut into 1-inch pieces
1 package (12 ounces) Cajun andouille or chili flavor chicken sausage, sliced ½ inch thick
½ cup chicken broth
1 can (28 ounces) crushed tomatoes with roasted garlic
¼ cup finely chopped green onions
1 bay leaf
½ teaspoon dried basil
½ teaspoon black pepper
¼ to ½ teaspoon red pepper flakes

Chicken Corn Chowder with Cheese

2 tablespoons butter or
   margarine
⅓ cup chopped celery
⅓ cup chopped red bell
   pepper
1½ tablespoons all-purpose
   flour
2 cups milk
1 can (14¾ ounces)
   cream-style corn
1⅓ cups *French's®* French
   Fried Onions, divided
1 cup diced cooked
   chicken
2 tablespoons chopped
   green chilies
½ cup (2 ounces) shredded
   Cheddar cheese

1. Melt butter in 3-quart saucepan over medium-high heat. Sauté celery and bell pepper 3 minutes or until crisp-tender. Blend in flour; cook 1 minute, stirring constantly. Gradually stir in milk and corn. Bring to a boil. Reduce heat; simmer 4 minutes or until thickened, stirring frequently.

2. Add ⅔ *cup* French Fried Onions, chicken and chilies. Cook until heated through. Spoon soup into serving bowls; sprinkle with remaining onions and cheese. Splash on **Frank's RedHot** Sauce to taste, if desired.

Makes 4 servings

Variation: For added Cheddar flavor, substitute **French's®** **Cheddar French Fried Onions** for the original flavor.

Prep Time: *5 minutes*
Cook Time: *10 minutes*

Chicken and Black Bean Chili

Slow Cooker Directions

1. Coat slow cooker with cooking spray. Combine chicken, chili powder, cumin and salt in slow cooker, tossing to coat. Add bell pepper, onion and garlic; mix well. Stir in tomatoes and salsa. Cover and cook 5 to 6 hours on LOW or 2½ to 3 hours on HIGH, or until chicken is no longer pink in center.

2. Turn heat to high; stir in beans. Cover and cook 5 to 10 minutes or until beans are heated through. Ladle into shallow bowls.　　*Makes 4 servings*

Serving Suggestion: Top this chunky chili with sour cream, diced ripe avocado, shredded Cheddar cheese, sliced green onions, chopped cilantro or crushed tortilla chips, if desired.

1 pound boneless skinless chicken thighs, cut into 1-inch chunks
2 teaspoons chili powder
2 teaspoons ground cumin
¾ teaspoon salt
1 green bell pepper, diced
1 small onion, chopped
3 cloves garlic, minced
1 can (14.5 ounces) diced tomatoes, undrained
1 cup chunky salsa
1 can (16 ounces) black beans, rinsed and drained

Chicken & Orzo Soup

Nonstick olive oil
  cooking spray
3 ounces boneless skinless
  chicken breast, cut
  into bite-size pieces
1 can (14½ ounces) fat-free
  reduced-sodium
  chicken broth
1 cup water
⅔ cup shredded carrot
⅓ cup sliced green onion
¼ cup uncooked orzo pasta
1 teaspoon grated fresh
  ginger
⅛ teaspoon ground turmeric
2 teaspoons lemon juice
  Dash black pepper
  Sliced green onions
  (optional)

1. Spray medium saucepan with cooking spray. Heat over medium-high heat. Add chicken. Cook and stir 2 to 3 minutes or until cooked through. Remove from saucepan and set aside.

2. In same saucepan, combine broth, water, carrot, green onion, orzo, ginger and turmeric. Bring to a boil. Reduce heat and simmer, covered, 8 to 10 minutes or until orzo is tender. Stir in chicken and lemon juice; cook until hot. Season to taste with pepper.

3. Ladle into serving bowls. Sprinkle with additional green onions, if desired.

Makes 2 servings

Simple Soups & Stews

Chicken Stew

Slow Cooker Directions

1. Combine chicken, tomatoes with juice, potatoes, okra and onion in slow cooker. Cover; cook on LOW 6 to 8 hours or until potatoes are tender.

2. Add corn, ketchup and barbecue sauce. Cover; cook on HIGH 30 minutes.

Makes 6 servings

Serving Suggestion: To complete this meal, serve with hot crusty rolls and a green salad.

4 to 5 cups chopped cooked chicken (about 5 boneless skinless chicken breasts)
1 can (28 ounces) whole tomatoes, undrained
2 large potatoes, cut into 1-inch pieces
½ pound okra, sliced
1 large onion, chopped
1 can (14 ounces) cream-style corn
½ cup ketchup
½ cup barbecue sauce

Main Dish Chicken Soup

1 can (49½ ounces) fat-free
    reduced-sodium
    chicken broth *or* 3 cans
    (14½ ounces each)
    fat-free reduced-sodium
    chicken broth plus
    6 ounces of water
1 cup grated carrots
½ cup sliced green onions
½ cup diced red bell
    pepper
½ cup frozen green peas
1 seedless cucumber
12 chicken tenders (about
    1 pound)
½ teaspoon white pepper

1. Place broth in large 4-quart Dutch oven. Bring to a boil over high heat. Add carrots, green onions, bell pepper and peas. Return to a boil. Reduce heat and simmer 3 minutes.

2. Meanwhile, cut ends off cucumber and discard. Using vegetable peeler, start at top and make long, noodle-like strips of cucumber. Slice any remaining cucumber pieces thinly with knife. Add cucumber to Dutch oven; cook 2 minutes over low heat.

3. Add chicken tenders and white pepper; simmer 5 minutes or until chicken is cooked through. *Makes 6 servings*

Serving Suggestion: Serve with a small mixed green salad or sliced tomatoes on a bed of lettuce and crusty French bread.

Chicken & White Bean Stew

In 12-inch skillet, heat olive oil over medium heat and cook carrots, onion and garlic, stirring occasionally, 5 minutes or until vegetables are tender. Stir in vinegar and cook 1 minute. Remove vegetables; set aside.

In same skillet, thoroughly brown chicken over medium-high heat. Return vegetables to skillet. Stir in Ragú Old World Style Pasta Sauce, beans and red pepper flakes. Bring to a boil over high heat. Reduce heat to medium and simmer covered, stirring occasionally, 15 minutes or until chicken is thoroughly cooked. Garnish, if desired, with fresh parsley and serve with toasted Italian bread.   *Makes 6 servings*

1 tablespoon olive oil
2 medium carrots, sliced (about 2 cups)
1 medium onion, thinly sliced
2 cloves garlic, finely chopped
1 tablespoon balsamic vinegar
1 pound boneless, skinless chicken breast halves or thighs, cut into chunks
1 jar (1 pound 10 ounces) RAGÚ® Old World Style® Pasta Sauce
2 cans (15 ounces each) cannellini or white kidney beans, rinsed and drained
Pinch crushed red pepper flakes (optional)

Chunky Chicken and Vegetable Soup

1 tablespoon canola oil
1 boneless skinless chicken
   breast (4 ounces), diced
½ cup chopped green bell
   pepper
½ cup thinly sliced celery
2 green onions, sliced
2 cans (14½ ounces each)
   chicken broth
1 cup water
½ cup sliced carrots
2 tablespoons cream
1 tablespoon finely
   chopped fresh parsley
¼ teaspoon dried thyme
⅛ teaspoon black pepper

1. Heat oil in large saucepan over medium heat. Add chicken; cook and stir 4 to 5 minutes or until cooked through. Add bell pepper, celery and onions. Cook and stir 7 minutes or until vegetables are tender.

2. Add broth, water, carrots, cream, parsley, thyme and black pepper. Simmer 10 minutes or until carrots are tender.   *Makes 4 servings*

Simple Soups & Stews

White Bean Chili

1. Spray large nonstick skillet with cooking spray; heat over medium heat until hot. Add chicken; cook and stir until browned, breaking into pieces. Remove chicken; drain fat from skillet.

2. Add celery, onions and garlic to skillet; cook and stir over medium heat 5 to 7 minutes or until tender. Sprinkle with chili powder, cumin, allspice, cinnamon and pepper; cook and stir 1 minute.

3. Return chicken to skillet. Stir in tomatoes with juice, beans and chicken broth; heat to a boil. Reduce heat to low and simmer, uncovered, 15 minutes breaking up tomatoes with back of spoon. Garnish as desired.

Makes 6 servings

Nonstick cooking spray
1 pound ground chicken
3 cups coarsely chopped celery
1½ cups coarsely chopped onions (about 2 medium)
3 cloves garlic, minced
4 teaspoons chili powder
1½ teaspoons ground cumin
¾ teaspoon ground allspice
¾ teaspoon ground cinnamon
½ teaspoon black pepper
1 can (16 ounces) whole tomatoes, undrained and coarsely chopped
1 can (15½ ounces) Great Northern beans, drained and rinsed
2 cups chicken broth

Thai Noodle Soup

1 package (3 ounces)
  ramen noodles
3/4 pound chicken tenders
2 cans (about 14 ounces
  each) chicken broth
1/4 cup shredded carrot
1/4 cup frozen snow peas
2 tablespoons thinly sliced
  green onions
1/2 teaspoon minced garlic
1/4 teaspoon ground ginger
3 tablespoons chopped
  fresh cilantro
1/2 lime, cut into 4 wedges

1. Break noodles into pieces. Cook noodles according to package directions (discard flavor packet). Drain and set aside.

2. Cut chicken tenders into 1/2-inch pieces. Combine chicken broth and chicken tenders in large saucepan or Dutch oven; bring to a boil over medium heat. Cook 2 minutes.

3. Add carrot, snow peas, green onions, garlic and ginger. Reduce heat to low; simmer 3 minutes. Add cooked noodles and cilantro; heat through. Serve soup with lime wedges.

Makes 4 servings

Prep and Cook Time: *15 minutes*

Simple Soups & Stews

Cajun Chili

1. Lightly brown sausage in large skillet over medium-high heat. Add chicken, onion and cayenne pepper; cook until browned. Drain.

2. Stir in remaining ingredients. Cook 5 minutes, stirring occasionally.

Makes 4 servings

Prep and Cook Time: *20 minutes*

6 ounces spicy sausage
   links, sliced
4 boneless, skinless chicken
   thighs, cut into cubes
1 medium onion, chopped
$\frac{1}{8}$ teaspoon cayenne pepper
1 can (15 ounces)
   black-eyed peas or
   kidney beans, drained
1 can (14½ ounces) DEL
   MONTE® Diced
   Tomatoes with Zesty
   Mild Green Chilies
1 medium green bell
   pepper, chopped

Quick Fix Dishes

Southwestern Chicken

1 cup prepared Italian
   salad dressing
1 tablespoon lime juice
1 tablespoon *French's®*
   Sweet & Tangy Honey
   Mustard
1 pound thinly sliced
   chicken cutlets
1⅓ cups *French's®* French
   Fried Onions
1 cup (4 ounces) shredded
   Cheddar cheese

1. Combine salad dressing, lime juice and mustard in small bowl. Pour marinade over chicken in deep dish. Cover and marinate in refrigerator 30 minutes or up to 1 hour.

2. Heat 3 tablespoons marinade in 12-inch nonstick skillet over high heat. Cook chicken 5 minutes or until chicken is no longer pink in center, turning once. (Discard remaining marinade.)

3. Sprinkle French Fried Onions and cheese over chicken. Cook, covered, 2 minutes or until cheese is melted. *Makes 4 servings*

Prep Time: *5 minutes*
Marinate Time: *30 minutes*
Cook Time: *7 minutes*

Savory Dill Chicken

2 tablespoons I CAN'T BELIEVE IT'S NOT BUTTER!® Spread
1½ pounds boneless, skinless chicken breast halves
1 cup water
1 package KNORR® Recipe Classics™ Vegetable or Spring Vegetable Soup, Dip and Recipe Mix
¼ teaspoon dried dill weed
½ cup sour cream

• In large skillet, melt I Can't Believe It's Not Butter!® Spread over medium-high heat and brown chicken, turning occasionally, 5 minutes.

• Stir in water, recipe mix and dill weed. Bring to a boil over high heat. Reduce heat to low and simmer covered, stirring occasionally, 10 minutes or until chicken is thoroughly cooked. Remove chicken to serving platter and keep warm.

• Remove skillet from heat; stir in sour cream. Spoon sauce over chicken and serve, if desired, with noodles.

Makes 4 to 6 servings

Prep Time: *5 minutes*
Cook Time: *16 minutes*

Quick Fix Dishes

Chili Cranberry Chicken

Combine first 4 ingredients; set aside. In large skillet, slowly brown chicken on both sides in oil. Pour reserved chili sauce mixture over chicken. Simmer, uncovered, 8 to 10 minutes or until chicken is cooked and sauce is of desired consistency, turning and basting occasionally.

Makes 4 to 6 servings and about 1 cup sauce

½ cup HEINZ® Chili Sauce
½ cup whole berry
   cranberry sauce
2 tablespoons orange
   marmalade
⅛ teaspoon ground allspice
4 to 6 skinless boneless
   chicken breast halves
   (about 1½ pounds)
2 teaspoons vegetable oil

Quick Fix Dishes

Caribbean Chutney Kabobs

20 (4-inch) bamboo skewers
½ medium pineapple
1 medium red bell pepper,
   cut into 1-inch pieces
¾ pound boneless skinless
   chicken breasts, cut
   into 1-inch pieces
½ cup bottled mango
   chutney
2 tablespoons orange juice
   or pineapple juice
1 teaspoon vanilla
¼ teaspoon ground nutmeg

1. To prevent burning, soak skewers in water at least 20 minutes before assembling kabobs.

2. Peel and core pineapple. Cut pineapple into 1-inch chunks. Alternately thread bell pepper, pineapple and chicken onto skewers. Place in shallow baking dish.

3. Combine chutney, orange juice, vanilla and nutmeg in small bowl; mix well. Pour over kabobs; cover. Refrigerate up to 4 hours.

4. Preheat broiler. Spray broiler pan with nonstick cooking spray. Place kabobs on prepared broiler pan; discard any leftover marinade. Broil kabobs 6 to 8 inches from heat 4 to 5 minutes on each side or until chicken is no longer pink in center. Transfer to serving plates.   *Makes 10 servings*

Quick Fix Dishes

Penne with Roasted Chicken & Vegetables

1. Remove chicken meat from bones and shred. Discard bones and skin.

2. Cook pasta according to package directions; drain and return to hot cooking pot. Add chicken and vegetables; toss together until dish is heated through. Sprinkle with cheese and season with pepper to taste.

Makes 6 servings

Tip: Cook twice as much pasta as you need one night and get a head start on the next pasta meal. Thoroughly drain the pasta you are not using immediately and plunge it into a bowl of ice water to stop the cooking. Drain completely and toss with 1 or 2 tablespoons of olive oil. Cover and refrigerate up to 3 days. To reheat the pasta, microwave on HIGH for 2 to 4 minutes, stirring halfway through.

1 whole roasted chicken (about 2 pounds)
1 box (16 ounces) penne pasta
1 pound roasted vegetables, cut into bite-size strips
1/3 cup shredded Parmesan cheese
   Freshly ground black pepper

Chicken Breasts Smothered in Tomatoes and Mozzarella

4 boneless skinless chicken
   breasts (about
   1½ pounds)
3 tablespoons olive oil,
   divided
1 cup chopped onions
2 teaspoons bottled
   minced garlic
1 can (14 ounces)
   Italian-style stewed
   tomatoes
1½ cups (6 ounces) shredded
   mozzarella cheese

1. Preheat broiler.

2. Pound chicken breasts between 2 pieces of plastic wrap to ¼-inch thickness using flat side of meat mallet or rolling pin.

3. Heat 2 tablespoons oil in ovenproof skillet over medium heat. Add chicken and cook about 3½ minutes per side or until no longer pink in center. Transfer to plate; cover and keep warm.

4. Heat remaining 1 tablespoon oil in same skillet over medium heat. Add onions and garlic; cook and stir 3 minutes. Add tomatoes; bring to a simmer. Return chicken to skillet, spooning onion and tomato mixture over chicken.

5. Sprinkle cheese over top. Broil 4 to 5 inches from heat until cheese is melted.   *Makes 4 servings*

Prep and Cook Time: *20 minutes*

Chicken and Asparagus Hollandaise

- Prepare hollandaise sauce according to package directions.

- Spray large skillet with nonstick cooking spray; cook chicken strips over medium-high heat 10 to 12 minutes or until browned, stirring occasionally.

- Add hollandaise sauce, lemon juice and asparagus.

- Cover and cook, stirring occasionally, 5 to 10 minutes or until asparagus is heated through. *Do not overcook.*

- Add cayenne pepper, salt and black pepper to taste.

Makes 4 to 6 servings

Serving Suggestion: Serve over rice or noodles.

Prep Time: *10 minutes*
Cook Time: *20 to 25 minutes*

1 package (1.25 ounces) hollandaise sauce mix
1 pound boneless skinless chicken breasts, cut into strips
2 teaspoons lemon juice
1 box (10 ounces) BIRDS EYE® frozen Asparagus
Dash cayenne pepper

Garden Ranch Linguine with Chicken

8 ounces linguine, cooked & drained

2 cups cooked mixed vegetables, such as broccoli, cauliflower and bell peppers

2 cups cubed cooked chicken

1 cup prepared HIDDEN VALLEY® The Original Ranch® Dressing

1 tablespoon grated Parmesan cheese

Combine all ingredients except cheese in a large saucepan; toss well. Heat through; sprinkle with cheese before serving.

Makes 4 servings

Tip: To save time, buy already cut-up vegetables from the salad bar. Steam or stir-fry them before completing this tasty recipe.

Quick Fix Dishes

Chicken and Mushrooms with Roasted Garlic Sauce

1. Heat olive oil in medium skillet over medium heat. Lightly brown chicken. Remove chicken from skillet and slice into thin strips. Return chicken to skillet.

2. Stir in pasta sauce and mushrooms. Simmer, covered, stirring occasionally, 10 minutes or until chicken is no longer pink in center.

3. Combine pasta and sauce mixture in large bowl. Sprinkle with Parmesan cheese. Garnish as desired.

Makes 4 servings

1 teaspoon olive oil
4 boneless skinless chicken breasts
1 jar (about 28 ounces) roasted garlic pasta sauce
1 cup sliced mushrooms
8 ounces corkscrew pasta, cooked and drained
Grated fresh Parmesan cheese

Classic Chicken Parmesan

6 boneless, skinless chicken breast halves, pounded thin (about 1½ pounds)
2 eggs, lightly beaten
1 cup Italian seasoned dry bread crumbs
2 tablespoons olive oil
1 jar (1 pound 10 ounces) RAGÚ® Old World Style® Pasta Sauce
1 cup shredded mozzarella cheese (about 4 ounces)

1. Preheat oven to 375°F. Dip chicken in eggs, then bread crumbs, coating well.

2. In 12-inch skillet, heat olive oil over medium-high heat and brown chicken; drain on paper towels.

3. In 11×7-inch baking dish, evenly spread 1 cup Ragú Old World Style Pasta Sauce. Arrange chicken in dish. Top with remaining sauce. Sprinkle with mozzarella cheese and, if desired, grated Parmesan cheese. Bake uncovered 25 minutes or until chicken is thoroughly cooked.   *Makes 6 servings*

Tip: To pound chicken, place a boneless, skinless breast between two sheets of waxed paper. Use a rolling pin to press down and out from the center to flatten.

Quick Fix Dishes

Chicken and Vegetable Pasta

1. Cook pasta according to package directions. Drain; place in large bowl. Cover to keep warm.

2. While pasta is cooking, combine vegetables, chicken and dressing in medium bowl; toss well. Grill or broil 6 to 8 minutes on each side or until vegetables are crisp-tender and chicken is no longer pink in center. (Vegetables may take less time than chicken.)

3. Cut vegetables and chicken into bite-size pieces. Add vegetables, chicken and pesto to pasta; toss well. *Makes 4 to 6 servings*

Prep and Cook Time: *20 minutes*

8 ounces (4 cups) uncooked bow tie pasta

2 red or green bell peppers, seeded and cut into quarters

1 medium zucchini, cut into halves

3 boneless skinless chicken breasts (about 1 pound)

½ cup Italian dressing

½ cup prepared pesto sauce

Garlic Chicken Melt

4 boneless, skinless chicken breast halves (about 1¼ pounds)

1 envelope LIPTON® RECIPE SECRETS® Savory Herb with Garlic Soup Mix

1 can (14 ounces) diced tomatoes, undrained *or* 1 large tomato, chopped

1 tablespoon BERTOLLI® Olive Oil

½ cup shredded mozzarella or Monterey Jack cheese (about 2 ounces)

1. Preheat oven to 375°F. In 13×9-inch baking or roasting pan, arrange chicken. Pour soup mix blended with tomatoes and oil over chicken.

2. Bake uncovered 25 minutes or until chicken is thoroughly cooked.

3. Sprinkle with mozzarella cheese and bake an additional 2 minutes or until cheese is melted.

Makes 4 servings

Pesto-Coated Baked Chicken

1. Preheat oven to 450°F. Arrange chicken in single layer in shallow baking pan. Combine pesto, sour cream and mayonnaise in small cup. Brush over chicken. Sprinkle with cheese and pine nuts.

2. Bake 8 to 10 minutes or until cooked through.   *Makes 4 servings*

Variation: Chicken can be cooked on an oiled grid over a preheated grill.

1 pound boneless skinless chicken breasts, cut into ½-inch thick cutlets
¼ cup plus 1 tablespoon prepared pesto
1½ teaspoons sour cream
1½ teaspoons mayonnaise
1 tablespoon shredded Parmesan cheese
1 tablespoon pine nuts

Quick Fix Dishes

Saucy Tomato Chicken

6 ounces uncooked yolk-free egg noodles

1 can (14½ ounces) stewed tomatoes with onions, celery and green bell pepper

2 cloves garlic, minced

1 teaspoon dried oregano
Nonstick cooking spray

4 boneless skinless chicken breasts, rinsed and patted dry, (4 ounces each)

2 teaspoons olive oil

1. Cook noodles according to package directions, omitting salt and oil; drain.

2. Meanwhile, heat large nonstick skillet over high heat; add tomatoes, garlic and oregano. Bring to a boil over high heat; boil 5 minutes, stirring constantly, or until liquid is reduced and tomato mixture becomes slightly darker in color. (Mixture will be thick.) Transfer to small bowl and keep warm. Wipe out skillet.

3. Spray same skillet with cooking spray. Add chicken and cook 6 minutes. Turn; reduce heat to medium-low. Spoon tomato mixture into skillet around chicken. Cover and cook 4 minutes or until chicken is no longer pink in center and juices run clear. Slice chicken into thin strips.

4. Remove skillet from heat. Place noodles on serving platter and top with chicken pieces. Add olive oil to tomato mixture in skillet and stir well to blend. Spoon equal amounts of tomato mixture over each piece of chicken.

Makes 4 servings

Dried Oregano

Spicy Chicken Stromboli

1. Preheat oven to 400°F. Coarsely chop broccoli. Combine broccoli, chicken, cheese, salsa and green onions in small bowl.

2. Unroll pizza dough. Pat into 15×10-inch rectangle. Sprinkle broccoli mixture evenly over top. Starting with long side, tightly roll into log jelly-roll style. Pinch seam to seal. Place on baking sheet, seam side down.

3. Bake 15 to 20 minutes or until golden brown. Transfer to wire rack to cool slightly. Slice and serve warm.

Makes 6 servings

Serving Suggestion: Serve with salsa on the side for dipping or pour salsa on top of slices for a boost of added flavor.

Prep and Cook Time: *30 minutes*

1 cup frozen broccoli
    florets, thawed
1 can (10 ounces) diced
    chicken
1½ cups (6 ounces) shredded
    Monterey Jack cheese
    with jalapeño peppers
¼ cup chunky salsa
2 green onions, chopped
1 can (10 ounces)
    refrigerated pizza
    dough

Sandwiches & Salads

Blackened Chicken Salad in Pitas

1 tablespoon paprika
1 teaspoon onion powder
½ teaspoon garlic powder
½ teaspoon dried oregano
½ teaspoon dried thyme
¼ teaspoon salt
¼ teaspoon white pepper
¼ teaspoon ground red
  pepper
¼ teaspoon black pepper
2 boneless skinless chicken
  breasts (about
  ¾ pound)
4 rounds pita bread
1 cup bite-size pieces
  spinach leaves
2 small tomatoes, cut into
  8 slices
8 thin slices cucumber
½ cup prepared reduced-fat
  ranch dressing

1. Combine paprika, onion powder, garlic powder, oregano, thyme, salt and red and black peppers in small bowl; rub on all surfaces of chicken. Grill chicken on covered grill over medium-hot coals 10 minutes per side or until chicken is no longer pink in center. Cool slightly. Cut into thin strips.

2. Wrap 2 pita bread rounds in paper towels. Microwave at HIGH 20 to 30 seconds or just until warm. Repeat with remaining pita breads. Cut in half horizantally.

3. Divide spinach, chicken strips, tomato slices, cucumber slices and ranch dressing among pita bread halves. Serve warm. *Makes 4 servings*

12 ounces chicken tenders
 Nonstick cooking spray
1 onion, thinly sliced
1 red bell pepper, cut into
 strips
½ cup zesty Italian dressing
¼ teaspoon red pepper
 flakes
4 pita bread rounds
8 leaves leaf lettuce
4 tablespoons crumbled
 feta cheese

Stir-Fry Pita Sandwiches

1. Cut chicken tenders in half lengthwise and crosswise. Coat large nonstick skillet with cooking spray. Cook and stir chicken over medium heat 3 minutes. Add onion and bell pepper; cook and stir 2 minutes. Add Italian dressing and red pepper flakes; cover and cook 3 minutes. Remove from heat; uncover and let cool 5 minutes.

2. While chicken mixture is cooling, cut pita breads in half to form pockets. Line each pocket with lettuce leaf. Spoon chicken filling into pockets; sprinkle with feta cheese.

Makes 4 servings

Prep and Cook Time: *17 minutes*

Sandwiches & Salads

Lemon Chicken Salad

1. Place cooking wine and chicken in large saucepan. Add enough water to cover. Bring to a boil; reduce heat. Simmer 10 minutes or until chicken is tender and cooked through. Let chicken cool in liquid for 45 minutes. Drain; cut chicken into bite-sized pieces.

2. In large bowl, combine chicken, snow peas, celery, scallions, mayonnaise, lemon peel and pepper. Cover and refrigerate 1 to 2 hours to blend flavors. Just before serving, stir in almonds. To serve, spoon chicken salad onto lettuce-lined plates.

Makes 4 servings

½ cup **HOLLAND HOUSE®** **White with Lemon Cooking Wine**
1 pound **boneless, skinless chicken breasts**
1 cup **snow peas, blanched, roughly chopped**
¾ cup **sliced celery**
¼ cup **sliced scallions**
½ cup **mayonnaise**
1 teaspoon **grated lemon peel**
 Black pepper, to taste
½ cup **toasted slivered almonds**
 Lettuce leaves, as needed

Easy Oriental Chicken Sandwiches

¼ cup peanut butter
2 tablespoons honey
2 tablespoons light soy
  sauce
½ teaspoon garlic powder
½ teaspoon ground ginger
4 boneless skinless chicken
  breasts (about
  1¼ pounds)
4 onion or Kaiser rolls,
  split
  Lettuce leaves
1 cup sliced cucumbers
1 cup bean sprouts
¼ cup sliced green onions

1. Preheat oven to 400°F. Combine peanut butter, honey, soy sauce, garlic powder and ginger in large bowl; stir until well blended. Reserve ¼ cup peanut butter mixture.

2. Place chicken on foil-lined baking pan. Spread remaining peanut butter mixture over chicken. Bake 20 minutes or until chicken is no longer pink in center.

3. Fill rolls with lettuce, cucumbers, bean sprouts and chicken; sprinkle with green onions. Serve with reserved peanut butter mixture.

Makes 4 servings

Sandwiches & Salads

Buffalo Chicken Salad Italiano

1. Combine Wing Sauce and salad dressing in bowl. Pour ½ cup mixture over chicken tenders in large bowl. Cover and refrigerate 20 minutes.

2. Cook chicken on electric grill pan or barbecue grill for 3 to 5 minutes until no longer pink in center.

3. Arrange salad greens, celery and cheese on serving plates. Top with chicken and drizzle with remaining Wing Sauce mixture.

Makes 4 servings

Tip: You may substitute 1 pound boneless, skinless chicken breast halves for chicken tenders.

Prep Time: *5 minutes*
Cook Time: *5 minutes*
Marinate Time: *20 minutes*

½ cup *Frank's® RedHot®* **Buffalo Wing Sauce**
½ cup **prepared Italian salad dressing**
1 pound **frozen chicken tenders, thawed**
8 cups **torn salad greens**
1 cup **sliced celery**
1 cup **crumbled gorgonzola or blue cheese**

Chicken and Pear Pita Pockets

3 cups diced cooked
   chicken
1 can (16 ounces) Bartlett
   Pear halves or slices,
   thoroughly drained
   and diced
¾ cup chopped celery
½ cup raisins or chopped
   dates
¼ cup each nonfat plain
   yogurt and lowfat
   mayonnaise
1 teaspoon each salt,
   lemon pepper and
   dried rosemary leaves,
   crushed
6 pita pocket bread, halved
12 lettuce leaves

Combine chicken, pears, celery and raisins in medium bowl. Prepare dressing by blending yogurt, mayonnaise, salt, lemon pepper and rosemary. Combine dressing and pear mixture; mix well. Refrigerate until serving. To serve, line each pita half with lettuce leaf. Portion ½ cup mixture into each half.

Makes 6 servings

Favorite Brand Name Recipe from Pacific Northwest Canned Pear Service

Sandwiches & Salads

Warm Ginger Almond Chicken Salad

1. In medium bowl, combine all dressing ingredients. Add chicken strips; blend well. Cover; refrigerate 1 to 2 hours. In serving bowl, combine greens, carrots, tomato halves and green onions. Refrigerate.

2. In large skillet, combine chicken and dressing. Bring to a boil, cooking and stirring until chicken is no longer pink in center, about 3 to 5 minutes. In small bowl, combine cornstarch and water; blend well. Stir into chicken mixture. Cook until mixture thickens, stirring constantly. Spoon hot chicken mixture over vegetables; toss to combine. Sprinkle with almonds. Serve immediately.

Makes 4 servings

DRESSING
- ⅓ cup **GRANDMA'S®** Molasses
- ¼ cup oil
- ¼ cup cider vinegar
- 1 teaspoon finely chopped ginger root *or* ½ teaspoon ground ginger
- 1 teaspoon soy sauce
- ½ teaspoon salt
- Dash hot pepper sauce

SALAD
- 1 pound boneless, skinless chicken breasts, cut into thin strips
- 4 cups, torn mixed greens
- 1 cup (2 medium) shredded carrots
- ½ cup cherry tomatoes, halved
- ¼ cup chopped green onions
- 1 tablespoon cornstarch
- 2 tablespoons water
- ¼ cup sliced almonds, toasted

Sandwiches & Salads

Open-Faced Italian Focaccia Sandwich

2 cups shredded cooked
   chicken
½ cup **HIDDEN VALLEY®**
   The Original Ranch®
   Dressing
¼ cup diagonally sliced
   green onions
1 piece focaccia bread,
   about ¾-inch thick,
   10×7-inches
2 medium tomatoes, thinly
   sliced
4 cheese slices, such as
   provolone, Cheddar or
   Swiss
2 tablespoons grated
   Parmesan cheese
   (optional)

Stir together chicken, dressing and onions in a small mixing bowl. Arrange chicken mixture evenly on top of focaccia. Top with layer of tomatoes and cheese slices. Sprinkle with Parmesan cheese, if desired. Broil 2 minutes or until cheese is melted and bubbly. *Makes 4 servings*

Note: Purchase rotisserie chicken at your favorite store to add great taste and save preparation time.

Sunburst Chicken Salad

Combine mayonnaise, sour cream, orange juice concentrate and orange peel in small bowl. Add chicken, kiwi, oranges and celery; toss to coat. Cover; refrigerate 2 hours. Serve on lettuce leaves. Sprinkle with cashews.

Makes 2 servings

1 tablespoon fat-free mayonnaise

1 tablespoon fat-free sour cream

2 teaspoons frozen orange juice concentrate, thawed

¼ teaspoon grated orange peel

1 boneless skinless chicken breast (about 1 pound), cooked and chopped

1 large kiwi, thinly sliced

⅓ cup canned mandarin oranges, drained

¼ cup finely chopped celery

4 lettuce leaves, washed

2 tablespoons coarsely chopped cashews

Chicken, Feta and Pepper Subs

1 pound boneless, skinless chicken breasts
3 tablespoons olive oil, divided
2 teaspoons TABASCO® brand Pepper Sauce
½ teaspoon salt
½ teaspoon ground cumin
1 red bell pepper, cut into strips
1 yellow or green bell pepper, cut into strips
½ cup crumbled feta cheese
4 (6-inch) French rolls

Cut chicken breasts into thin strips. Heat 1 tablespoon oil in 12-inch skillet over medium-high heat. Add chicken; cook until well browned on all sides, stirring frequently. Stir in TABASCO® Sauce, salt and cumin. Remove mixture to medium bowl. Add remaining 2 tablespoons oil to same skillet over medium heat. Add bell peppers; cook about 5 minutes or until tender-crisp, stirring occasionally. Toss with chicken and feta cheese.

To serve, cut rolls crosswise in half. Cover bottom halves with chicken mixture and top with remaining roll halves. *Makes 4 servings*

Garden Pasta Salad

Combine pasta, chicken, onion, bell pepper, zucchini, olives, red pepper flakes and salt in large bowl; toss lightly. Combine soup and lemon juice in small bowl; mix well. Pour soup mixture over pasta salad; mix well. Sprinkle with Parmesan cheese, basil and parsley, if desired.   *Makes 8 servings*

6 cups cooked penne pasta
2 cups shredded cooked skinless chicken breast
¾ cup chopped red onion
¾ cup chopped red or green bell pepper
¾ cup sliced zucchini
1 can (4 ounces) sliced black olives, drained
1 teaspoon red pepper flakes
1 teaspoon salt
1 can (10¾ ounces) condensed cream of chicken soup, undiluted
½ cup lemon juice
½ cup grated Parmesan cheese
½ cup chopped fresh basil
¼ cup chopped fresh parsley (optional)

½ cup mayonnaise
¼ teaspoon garlic powder
½ teaspoon black pepper, divided
1 loaf (16 ounces) focaccia or Italian bread
4 boneless skinless chicken breasts (about 1¼ pounds)
3 tablespoons olive oil
2 cloves garlic, minced
1½ teaspoons dried basil
½ teaspoon salt
1 green bell pepper, cut into quarters
1 medium zucchini, cut lengthwise into 4 slices
2 Italian plum tomatoes, sliced

Dried Oregano

Basil Chicken and Vegetables on Focaccia

1. Combine mayonnaise, garlic powder and ¼ teaspoon black pepper in small bowl; set aside. Cut focaccia into quarters. Cut each quarter horizontally in half; set aside.

2. Combine chicken, oil, garlic, basil, salt and remaining ¼ teaspoon black pepper in large resealable plastic food storage bag. Seal bag; knead to combine. Add bell pepper and zucchini; knead to coat.

3. Grill or broil chicken, bell pepper and zucchini 4 inches from heat 6 to 8 minutes on each side or until chicken is no longer pink in center. (Bell pepper and zucchini may take less time.)

4. Top bottom half of each focaccia quarter with mayonnaise mixture, tomatoes, bell pepper, zucchini and chicken. Top with focaccia tops.

Makes 4 servings

Sandwiches & Salads

Hula Chicken Salad with Orange Poppy Seed Dressing

1. Combine salad dressing, mustard, orange peel, water and poppy seeds; mix well. Reserve.

2. Rub chicken tenders with jerk seasoning. Skewer chicken and grill over medium-high heat until no longer pink, about 5 minutes per side.

3. Arrange lettuce and fruit on salad plates. Top with chicken and serve with dressing. *Makes 4 servings*

Prep Time: 15 minutes
Cook Time: 10 minutes

½ cup prepared vinaigrette salad dressing
¼ cup *French's®* Honey Dijon Mustard
1 tablespoon grated orange peel
1 tablespoon water
1 teaspoon poppy seeds
1 pound chicken tenders
1 tablespoon jerk seasoning
8 cups cut-up romaine lettuce
3 cups cut-up fruit from salad bar such as oranges, melon, strawberries, pineapple

Glazed Teriyaki Chicken Stir-Fry Sub

¼ cup *French's®* Honey Dijon Mustard

2 tablespoons teriyaki sauce

1 tablespoon sucralose sugar substitute

1 tablespoon grated, peeled ginger root

1 tablespoon cider or red wine vinegar

1 tablespoon vegetable oil

1 pound boneless skinless chicken, cut into thin strips

1 cup coarsely chopped red or yellow bell peppers

½ cup each coarsely chopped red onion and plum tomatoes

4 Italian hero rolls, split (about 8 inches each)

2 cups shredded Napa cabbage or romaine lettuce

1. Combine mustard, teriyaki sauce, sugar substitute, ginger and vinegar in small bowl; set aside.

2. Heat oil in large skillet or wok over high heat. Stir-fry chicken 5 minutes until no longer pink. Add vegetables and stir-fry 2 minutes until just tender. Pour sauce mixture over stir-fry and cook 1 minute.

3. Arrange cabbage on rolls and top with equal portions of stir-fry. Close rolls. Serve warm.   *Makes 4 servings*

Prep Time: *10 minutes*
Cook Time: *8 minutes*

Cobb Salad

1. Place lettuce in salad bowl.

2. Dice chicken; place in center of lettuce.

3. Arrange tomato, bacon and avocado in rows on either side of chicken.

4. Drizzle with dressing. Serve immediately.

Makes 4 main-dish or 8 side-dish servings

Serving Suggestion: Serve with warm French or Italian rolls.

Prep Time: *15 minutes*

1 package (10 ounces) torn mixed salad greens *or* 8 cups torn romaine lettuce

6 ounces deli chicken, turkey or smoked turkey breast, cut ¼ inch thick

1 large tomato, seeded and chopped

⅓ cup bacon bits or crisp-cooked bacon, crumbled

1 large ripe avocado, peeled and diced

⅓ cup prepared blue cheese or Caesar salad dressing

Mediterranean Grilled Chicken Wraps

½ cup *French's®*
Gourmayo™
Sun Dried Tomato
Light Mayonnaise
1 package (4 ounces) goat
cheese, at room
temperature
½ cup chopped Spanish
olives
5 (10-inch) flour tortillas
2½ cups shredded romaine
lettuce
1 pound boneless, skinless
chicken breasts; grilled
and cut into strips

1. Combine mayonnaise and goat cheese; beat or whisk until smooth. Stir in olives.

2. Spread about 3 tablespoons cheese mixture evenly on each tortilla. Top with lettuce and chicken, dividing evenly. Roll up tightly. Cut in half to serve.

Makes 5 servings

Tip: Serve this spread with grilled burgers or on roast beef sandwiches. Also great with grilled vegetables.

Prep Time: *15 minutes*

Sandwiches & Salads

Light & Easy Chicken Salad

1. Whisk together salad dressing, mustard, orange juice and peel in large bowl. Add chicken and vegetables; toss gently until evenly coated. Season to taste with salt and pepper.

2. Cover; chill in refrigerator 30 minutes. Serve over salad greens or in sandwiches, as desired.

Makes 6 servings

Prep Time: *30 minutes*
Chill Time: *30 minutes*

½ cup low-fat Italian salad dressing
¼ cup *French's®* Bold n' Spicy Brown Mustard
¼ cup orange juice
1 teaspoon grated orange peel
3 cups (12 ounces) sliced cooked chicken
1½ cups frozen whole green beans, thawed and drained
½ pound red potatoes, cooked and cut into ½-inch wedges
½ cup sliced celery
½ cup sliced red onion

Apricot Chicken Sandwiches

6 ounces poached chicken
   tenders
2 tablespoons apricot
   spread
2 tablespoons chopped
   fresh apricots (pits
   removed)
4 slices whole wheat bread
4 lettuce leaves

1. Drain cooked chicken; chop well. Mix with apricot spread and chopped fruit.

2. Top bread with lettuce leaves. Divide chicken mixture evenly among bread slices; slice in half, folding over to make a half-sandwich. Slice each half again to make 2 wedges. Serve immediately. *Makes 4 servings*

Napa Valley Chicken Salad

Combine chicken, grapes, celery, pecans and onions in a medium bowl. Stir together dressing and mustard; toss with salad. Cover and refrigerate for 2 hours.   *Makes 4 servings*

2 cups diced cooked chicken
1 cup seedless red grapes, halved
1 cup diced celery
½ cup chopped toasted pecans
¼ cup thinly sliced green onions
½ cup HIDDEN VALLEY® The Original Ranch® Dressing
1 teaspoon Dijon mustard

Pesto Chicken & Pepper Wraps

⅔ cup refrigerated or frozen pesto sauce, thawed and divided

3 tablespoons red wine vinegar

¼ teaspoon salt

¼ teaspoon black pepper

1¼ pounds skinless boneless chicken thighs or breasts

2 red bell peppers, cut in half, stemmed and seeded

5 (8-inch) flour tortillas

5 thin slices (3-inch rounds) fresh-pack mozzarella cheese*

5 leaves Boston or red leaf lettuce

Orange slices

Red and green chilies

Fresh basil sprigs

*Packaged sliced whole milk or part-skim mozzarella cheese can be substituted for fresh-pack mozzarella cheese.

Combine ¼ cup pesto, vinegar, salt and black pepper in medium bowl. Add chicken; toss to coat. Cover and refrigerate at least 30 minutes. Remove chicken from marinade; discard marinade. Grill chicken over medium-hot KINGSFORD® Briquets about 4 minutes per side until chicken is no longer pink in center, turning once. Grill bell peppers, skin sides down, about 8 minutes until skin is charred. Place bell peppers in large resealable plastic food storage bag; seal. Let stand 5 minutes; remove skin. Cut chicken and bell peppers into thin strips. Spread about 1 tablespoon of remaining pesto down center of each tortilla; top with chicken, bell peppers, cheese and lettuce. Roll tortillas to enclose filling. Garnish with orange slices, chiles and basil sprigs.

Makes 5 wraps

Sandwiches & Salads

Tropical Curried Chicken Salad

1. Place salad dressing, Worcestershire, honey, **Frank's® RedHot®** Sauce, curry and garlic in blender or food processor. Cover; process until well blended. Reserve ½ cup curry mixture to dress salad.

2. Place chicken in large resealable plastic food storage bag. Pour remaining curry mixture over chicken. Seal bag; marinate in refrigerator 30 minutes.

3. Heat electric grill pan or barbecue grill. Grill chicken 10 to 15 minutes or until no longer pink in center. Arrange salad greens on large serving platter. Cut chicken into thin slices. Arrange over greens. Top with nuts and coconut. Serve with reserved dressing. *Makes 4 servings*

Prep Time: *15 minutes*
Cook Time: *15 minutes*
Marinate Time: *30 minutes*

⅔ cup prepared olive oil vinaigrette salad dressing
¼ cup *French's®* Worcestershire Sauce
¼ cup honey
2 tablespoons *Frank's® RedHot®* Cayenne Pepper Sauce
2 teaspoons curry powder
2 cloves garlic, minced
1 pound boneless, skinless chicken breasts
8 cups washed and torn watercress and Boston lettuce
¼ cup coarsely chopped unsalted cashew nuts
½ cup shredded coconut, toasted

Mustard-Glazed Chicken Sandwiches

½ cup honey-mustard
barbecue sauce,
divided
4 Kaiser rolls, split
4 boneless skinless chicken
breast (1 pound)
4 slices Swiss cheese
4 leaves leaf lettuce
8 slices tomato

1. Spread about 1 teaspoon barbecue sauce on cut sides of each roll.

2. Pound chicken breast halves between 2 pieces of plastic wrap to ½-inch thickness with flat side of meat mallet or rolling pin. Spread remaining barbecue sauce over chicken.

3. Cook chicken in large nonstick skillet over medium-low heat 5 minutes per side or until no longer pink in center. Remove skillet from heat. Place cheese slices on chicken; let stand 3 minutes to melt.

4. Place lettuce leaves and tomato slices on roll bottoms; top with chicken and roll tops.

Makes 4 servings

Serving Suggestion: Serve sandwiches with yellow tomatoes, baby carrots and celery sticks.

Prep and Cook Time: *19 minutes*

Sandwiches & Salads

Chicken and Spinach Salad

1. Cut chicken into 2×½-inch strips. Spray large nonstick skillet with cooking spray; heat over medium heat until hot. Add chicken; cook and stir 5 minutes or until no longer pink in center. Remove from skillet; set aside.

2. Divide spinach, lettuce, grapefruit, onion, cheese and chicken among 4 salad plates. Combine citrus blend concentrate and Italian dressing in small bowl; drizzle over salads. Garnish with assorted greens, if desired.

Makes 4 servings

¾ **pound chicken tenders**
   Nonstick cooking spray
4 **cups washed, stemmed**
   and shredded spinach
2 **cups washed and torn**
   romaine lettuce
1 **large grapefruit, peeled**
   and sectioned
8 **thin slices red onion,**
   separated into rings
2 **tablespoons (½ ounce)**
   crumbled blue cheese
½ **cup frozen citrus blend**
   concentrate, thawed
¼ **cup prepared fat-free**
   Italian salad dressing
   Assorted fresh greens for
   garnish (optional)

Sandwiches & Salads

Asian Wraps

Nonstick cooking spray
8 ounces boneless skinless chicken breasts or thighs, cut into ½-inch pieces
1 teaspoon minced fresh ginger
1 teaspoon minced fresh garlic
¼ teaspoon red pepper flakes
¼ cup reduced-sodium teriyaki sauce
4 cups (about 8 ounces) packaged coleslaw mix
½ cup sliced green onions
4 (10-inch) flour tortillas
8 teaspoons plum fruit spread

1. Spray nonstick wok or large skillet with cooking spray; heat over medium-high heat. Stir-fry chicken 2 minutes. Add ginger, garlic and pepper flakes; stir-fry 2 minutes. Add teriyaki sauce; mix well.* Add cole slaw mix and green onions; stir-fry 4 minutes or until chicken is no longer pink and cabbage is crisp-tender.

2. Spread each tortilla with 2 teaspoons fruit spread; evenly spoon chicken mixture down center of tortillas. Roll up to form wraps.

Makes 4 servings

If sauce is too thick, add up to 2 tablespoons water to thin it.

Prep Time: 10 minutes
Cook Time: 10 minutes

Sandwiches & Salads

Monterey Chicken Sandwiches

1. Heat oil and butter in large skillet over medium heat. Add chicken; sprinkle with thyme. Cook 8 minutes or until browned on both sides and no longer pink in center, turning after 4 minutes. Season with salt and pepper to taste. Remove from skillet; keep warm.

2. Add onion to skillet; cook until tender.

3. Fill rolls with radicchio leaves, chicken and onions. Serve with mango chutney and olives, if desired.   *Makes 4 sandwiches*

Serving Suggestion: Serve with corn on the cob.

1 tablespoon oil
1 tablespoon butter
4 boneless skinless chicken breast (about 1 pound)
1 teaspoon dried thyme
   Salt and pepper
1 large red onion, thinly sliced
4 Kaiser rolls, split
   Radicchio or lettuce leaves

Outrageous Mexican Chicken Salad

6 cups shredded lettuce
1 bag (9 ounces) tortilla chips, crushed (about 3 cups)
2 cups cubed cooked chicken
1 can (15½ ounces) kidney beans, rinsed and drained
1½ cups prepared HIDDEN VALLEY® The Original Ranch® Dressing
½ cup (2 ounces) shredded Cheddar cheese
Tomatoes and olives

Combine lettuce, tortilla chips, chicken, beans, dressing and cheese in a large bowl. Garnish with tomatoes and olives. *Makes 4 to 6 servings*

Chicken and Mozzarella Melts

1. Preheat oven to 350°F. Rub garlic on all surfaces of chicken. Spray medium nonstick skillet with cooking spray; heat over medium heat until hot. Add chicken; cook 5 to 6 minutes on each side or until no longer pink in center. Sprinkle with salt and pepper.

2. Brush pesto sauce onto bottom halves of rolls; layer with spinach, basil, if desired, and tomatoes. Place chicken in rolls; sprinkle cheese evenly over chicken. (If desired, sandwiches may be prepared up to this point and wrapped in aluminum foil. Refrigerate until ready to bake. Bake in preheated 350°F oven until chicken is warm, about 20 minutes.)

3. Wrap sandwiches in aluminum foil; bake about 10 minutes or until cheese is melted.

Makes 4 servings

2 cloves garlic, crushed
4 boneless skinless chicken breasts (about 1 pound)
Nonstick cooking spray
⅛ teaspoon salt
⅛ teaspoon black pepper
1 tablespoon prepared pesto sauce
4 small hard rolls, split
12 fresh spinach leaves
8 fresh basil leaves* (optional)
3 plum tomatoes, sliced
½ cup (2 ounces) shredded part-skim mozzarella cheese

*Omit basil leaves if fresh are unavailable. Do not substitute dried basil leaves.

Sizzling Stirfry

Easy Make-at-Home Chinese Chicken

3 tablespoons frozen
   orange juice
   concentrate, thawed
2 tablespoons reduced-
   sodium soy sauce
2 tablespoons water
¾ teaspoon cornstarch
¼ teaspoon garlic powder
2 carrots, peeled
1 (12-ounce) package
   cut-up broccoli and
   cauliflower florets
   Nonstick cooking spray
2 teaspoons canola oil
¾ pound boneless skinless
   chicken breasts, cut
   into bite-size pieces
1⅓ cups hot cooked rice

1. For sauce, stir together orange juice concentrate, soy sauce, water, cornstarch and garlic powder; set aside.

2. Use bottle opener or ice pick to make 4 to 5 lengthwise cuts down each carrot, not cutting completely through carrot. Cut crosswise into ¼-inch-thick slices, forming flowers.

3. Spray nonstick wok or large skillet with cooking spray. Add carrots to wok. Stir-fry over high heat 1 minute. Add broccoli and cauliflower to wok. Stir-fry 2 to 3 minutes or until vegetables are crisp-tender. Remove vegetables from wok or skillet; set aside.

4. Add oil to wok. Stir-fry chicken in hot oil 2 to 3 minutes or until cooked through. Push chicken to sides of wok. Add sauce mixture; cook and stir until boiling. Return all vegetables to wok; cook and stir until mixture is heated through. Serve with hot cooked rice. *Makes 4 servings*

Chicken and Asparagus Stir-Fry

1 cup uncooked rice
2 tablespoons vegetable oil
1 pound boneless skinless chicken breasts, cut into ½-inch-wide strips
2 medium red bell peppers, cut into thin strips
½ pound fresh asparagus,* cut diagonally into 1-inch pieces
½ cup stir-fry sauce

*For stir-frying, select thin stalks of asparagus and cut them on the diagonal—they will cook more quickly.

1. Cook rice according to package directions. Keep hot.

2. Heat oil in wok or large skillet over medium-high heat until hot. Stir-fry chicken 3 to 4 minutes or until chicken is no longer pink in center.

3. Stir in bell peppers and asparagus; reduce heat to medium. Cover and cook 2 minutes or until vegetables are crisp-tender, stirring once or twice.

4. Stir in sauce; heat through. Serve over rice.   *Makes 4 servings*

Prep and Cook Time: *18 minutes*

Sausage and Chicken Jambalaya Stir-Fry

1. Cook rice according to package directions. Set aside.

2. Heat oil in wok or large skillet over medium-high heat until hot. Stir-fry chicken 2 minutes. Add sausage; stir-fry until sausage and chicken are brown, about 4 minutes. Remove from wok to medium bowl.

3. Add onion and bell pepper to wok; reduce heat to low. Cover and cook 2 to 3 minutes, stirring once or twice. Stir in garlic; cook, uncovered, 1 minute more.

4. Add tomatoes, sausage, chicken, broth, parsley, thyme, salt, black pepper and red pepper. Bring to a boil. Reduce heat to medium-low. Simmer, uncovered, 5 minutes or until most liquid has evaporated. Stir in rice; heat through.   *Makes 4 servings*

Prep and Cook Time: *30 minutes*

1 cup uncooked rice
1 teaspoon vegetable oil
¼ pound chicken tenders, cut into 1-inch pieces
½ pound Andouille sausage, cut into bite-size pieces
1 large onion, chopped
¾ cup chopped green bell pepper
1 teaspoon bottled minced garlic
1 can (15½ ounces) diced canned tomatoes, drained
½ cup chicken broth
1 tablespoon dried parsley flakes
½ teaspoon dried thyme
¼ teaspoon salt
¼ teaspoon black pepper
⅛ to ¼ teaspoon ground red pepper

Chicken and Vegetables with Mustard Sauce

1 tablespoon sugar
2 teaspoons cornstarch
1½ teaspoons dry mustard
2 tablespoons soy sauce
2 tablespoons water
2 tablespoons rice vinegar
1 pound boneless skinless chicken breasts
4 teaspoons vegetable oil, divided
2 cloves garlic, minced
1 small red bell pepper, cut into short thin strips
½ cup thinly sliced celery
1 small onion, cut into thin wedges
3 cups hot cooked Chinese egg noodles (3 ounces uncooked)

1. Combine sugar, cornstarch and mustard in small bowl. Blend soy sauce, water and vinegar into cornstarch mixture until smooth. Cut chicken into 1-inch pieces.

2. Heat 2 teaspoons oil in wok or large nonstick skillet over medium heat. Add chicken and garlic; stir-fry 3 minutes or until chicken is cooked through. Remove and reserve.

3. Add remaining 2 teaspoons oil to wok. Add bell pepper, celery and onion; stir-fry 3 minutes or until vegetables are crisp-tender.

4. Stir soy sauce mixture; add to wok. Cook and stir 30 seconds or until sauce boils and thickens.

5. Return chicken with any accumulated juices to wok; heat through. Serve over Chinese noodles. Garnish with celery leaves, if desired.

Makes 4 servings

Thai Curry Stir-Fry

1. Stir together broth, cornstarch, soy sauce, curry powder and red pepper. Set aside.

2. Spray nonstick wok or large nonstick skillet with cooking spray. Heat over medium-high heat. Add onions and garlic; stir-fry 1 minute. Remove from wok.

3. Add broccoli and carrot to wok; stir-fry 2 to 3 minutes or until crisp-tender. Remove from wok.

4. Add oil to hot wok. Add chicken and stir-fry 2 to 3 minutes or until cooked through. Stir broth mixture. Add to wok. Cook and stir until broth mixture comes to a boil and thickens slightly. Return all vegetables to wok. Heat through. Serve over rice. *Makes 2 servings*

½ cup fat-free reduced-sodium chicken broth
2 teaspoons cornstarch
2 teaspoons reduced-sodium soy sauce
1½ teaspoons curry powder
⅛ teaspoon red pepper flakes
Nonstick olive oil cooking spray
3 green onions, sliced
2 cloves garlic, minced
2 cups broccoli florets
⅔ cup sliced carrot
1½ teaspoons olive oil
6 ounces boneless skinless chicken breasts, cut into bite-size pieces
⅔ cup hot cooked rice, prepared without salt

Sizzling Stirfry

Golden Chicken Stir-Fry

½ pound chicken tenders, cut into thin strips

½ cup stir-fry sauce, divided

3 tablespoons vegetable oil, divided

1 medium onion, thinly sliced

1 clove garlic, minced

2 carrots, cut diagonally into thin slices

1 rib celery, cut diagonally into thin slices

1 tablespoon sesame seeds, toasted

½ teaspoon five-spice powder

¼ teaspoon dark sesame oil

2 cups hot cooked white rice

Toss chicken with 2 tablespoons stir-fry sauce in small bowl. Heat 1 tablespoon vegetable oil in hot wok or large skillet over medium-high heat. Add chicken and stir-fry 2 minutes; remove and set aside. Heat remaining 2 tablespoons vegetable oil in same pan. Add onion; stir-fry 2 minutes. Add garlic, carrots and celery; stir-fry 2 minutes longer. Add remaining stir-fry sauce, chicken, sesame seeds and five-spice powder to pan. Cook and stir until chicken and vegetables are coated with sauce. Remove from heat; stir in sesame oil. Serve with rice.

Makes 4 servings

Chicken with Walnuts

1. Cook rice according to package directions.

2. Combine broth, plum sauce, soy sauce and cornstarch in small bowl; set aside.

3. Heat 1 tablespoon oil in wok or large skillet over medium-high heat. Add peppers and onions; stir-fry 3 minutes or until crisp-tender. Remove vegetables from wok. Drain; discard liquid.

4. Heat remaining 1 tablespoon oil in same wok. Add chicken and garlic; stir-fry 3 minutes or until chicken is cooked through.

5. Stir broth mixture; add to wok. Cook and stir 1 minute or until sauce thickens. Stir in vegetables and walnuts; cook 1 minute more. Serve over rice.

Makes 4 servings

Prep and Cook time: *19 minutes*

1 cup uncooked instant rice
½ cup chicken broth
¼ cup Chinese plum sauce
2 tablespoons soy sauce
2 teaspoons cornstarch
2 tablespoons vegetable oil, divided
3 cups frozen bell peppers and onions
1 pound boneless skinless chicken breasts, cut into ¼-inch strips
1 clove garlic, minced
1 cup walnut halves

Sizzling Stirfry

Honey Mustard BBQ Chicken Stir-Fry

1 box (10 ounces)
   couscous pasta
1 pound boneless skinless
   chicken, cut into strips
1 medium red bell pepper,
   cut into thin strips
1 medium onion, sliced
⅓ cup *French's®* Sweet &
   Tangy Honey Mustard
⅓ cup barbecue sauce

1. Prepare couscous according to package directions. Keep warm. Heat *1 tablespoon oil* in large nonstick skillet over medium-high heat. Cook and stir chicken in batches 5 to 10 minutes or until browned. Transfer to bowl. Drain fat.

2. Heat *1 tablespoon oil* in same skillet until hot. Cook and stir vegetables 3 minutes or until crisp-tender. Return chicken to skillet. Stir in *⅔ cup water,* mustard and barbecue sauce. Heat to boiling, stirring often. Serve over couscous.

Makes 4 servings

Prep Time: *10 minutes*
Cook Time: *15 minutes*

Sizzling Stirfry

Chicken Chow Mein

1. Toss chicken with garlic in small bowl.

2. Heat ½ teaspoon vegetable oil in wok or large nonstick skillet over medium-high heat. Add chicken mixture; stir-fry 3 minutes or until chicken is no longer pink. Transfer to medium bowl; toss with soy sauce and sherry.

3. Heat remaining ½ teaspoon vegetable oil in wok. Add snow peas; stir-fry 1 minute. Add green onions; stir-fry 30 seconds. Add chicken mixture; stir-fry 1 minute.

4. Add noodles to wok; stir-fry 2 minutes or until heated through. Stir in sesame oil, if desired. Garnish with cherry tomatoes and fresh herbs, if desired.

Makes 4 servings

1 pound boneless skinless chicken breasts, cut into thin strips

2 cloves garlic, minced

1 teaspoon vegetable oil, divided

2 tablespoons reduced-sodium soy sauce

2 tablespoons dry sherry

1 package (6 ounces) frozen snow peas, thawed

3 large green onions, cut diagonally into 1-inch pieces

4 ounces uncooked Chinese egg noodles or vermicelli, cooked, drained

1 teaspoon dark sesame oil (optional)

Sizzling Stirfry

Pineapple Basil Chicken Supreme

1 can (8 ounces) pineapple
   chunks in unsweetened
   juice
2 teaspoons cornstarch
3 boneless skinless chicken
   breast halves (about
   1 pound)
2 tablespoons peanut oil
2 to 4 red serrano
   peppers,* cut into thin
   strips (optional)
2 cloves garlic, minced
2 green onions, cut into
   1-inch pieces
¾ cup roasted, unsalted
   cashews
¼ cup chopped fresh basil
   (do not use dried)
1 tablespoon fish sauce**
1 tablespoon soy sauce
   Hot cooked rice
   Kumquat flower for
   garnish

*Serrano peppers can sting and irritate
the skin; wear rubber gloves when
handling peppers and do not touch
eyes. Wash hands after handling.

**Fish sauce is available at most large
supermarkets and Asian markets.

1. Drain pineapple, reserving juice. Combine reserved juice and cornstarch in small bowl; set aside.

2. Cut chicken into ¾-inch pieces. Heat wok over high heat 1 minute or until hot. Drizzle oil into wok and heat 30 seconds. Add chicken, peppers and garlic; stir-fry 3 minutes or until chicken is no longer pink. Add green onions; stir-fry 1 minute. Stir cornstarch mixture; add to wok. Cook 1 minute or until thickened. Add pineapple, cashews, basil, fish sauce and soy sauce; stir-fry 1 minute or until heated through. Serve over rice and garnish, if desired.

Makes 4 servings

Chicken Stir-Fry

- Cut chicken into ½-inch-thick long strips.

- In wok or large skillet, heat oil over medium-high heat.

- Add chicken; cook 5 minutes, stirring occasionally.

- Meanwhile, in small bowl, combine orange juice, soy sauce and cornstarch; blend well and set aside.

- Add vegetables to chicken; cook 5 minutes more or until chicken is no longer pink in center, stirring occasionally.

- Stir in soy sauce mixture; cook 1 minute or until heated through.

Makes 4 servings

Serving Suggestion: Serve over hot cooked rice.

Birds Eye Idea: When cooking rice, add one teaspoon lemon juice to each quart of water you use so the grains will stay white and separate.

Prep Time: *5 minutes*
Cook Time: *12 minutes*

4 boneless skinless chicken breast halves (about 1½ pounds)
2 tablespoons vegetable oil
2 tablespoons orange juice
2 tablespoons light soy sauce
1 tablespoon cornstarch
1 bag (16 ounces) BIRDS EYE® frozen Farm Fresh Mixtures Broccoli, Carrots & Water Chestnuts

Sizzling Stirfry

Mandarin Orange Chicken

2 tablespoons rice vinegar

2 tablespoons soy sauce

2 tablespoons olive oil, divided

2 teaspoons grated orange peel

1 clove garlic, minced

1 pound boneless skinless chicken breasts, cut into strips

2 cans (11 ounces each) mandarin oranges, undrained

½ cup (approximately) orange juice

2 tablespoons cornstarch

½ teaspoon red pepper flakes

1 onion, cut into thin wedges

1 small zucchini, cut into halves and sliced diagonally

1 small yellow squash, cut into halves and sliced diagonally

1 red bell pepper, cut into 1-inch triangles

1. Combine vinegar, soy sauce, 1 tablespoon oil, orange peel and garlic in medium bowl. Add chicken; toss to coat well. Cover and refrigerate 15 minutes to 1 hour.

2. Drain chicken, reserving marinade. Drain oranges, reserving liquid; set oranges aside. Combine marinade from chicken and liquid from oranges in small bowl; add enough orange juice to make 2 cups liquid. Whisk in cornstarch and red pepper flakes; set aside.

3. Heat remaining 1 tablespoon oil in wok or large skillet over high heat. Add chicken; stir-fry 2 to 3 minutes or until no longer pink. Remove chicken; set aside.

4. Stir-fry onion 1 minute over high heat. Add zucchini and squash; stir-fry 1 minute. Add bell pepper; stir-fry 1 minute or until all vegetables are crisp-tender. Add orange juice mixture. Cook and stir until mixture comes to a boil; boil 1 minute. Add chicken, cooking until hot. Add oranges and gently stir. Transfer to serving plate. Serve with rice, if desired.

Makes 6 servings

Shanghai Chicken with Asparagus and Ham

1. To blanch asparagus pieces, cook 3 minutes in enough boiling water to cover. Plunge asparagus into cold water. Drain well.

2. Heat oil in large nonstick skillet over medium heat. Add onion and garlic; stir-fry 2 minutes. Add chicken; stir-fry 2 minutes. Add asparagus; stir-fry 2 minutes or until chicken is cooked through.

3. Add teriyaki sauce; mix well. Add ham; stir-fry until heated through. Serve over noodles. Garnish with carrot strips and fresh herbs, if desired.

Makes 4 servings

2 cups diagonally cut 1-inch asparagus pieces*
1 pound boneless skinless chicken breasts, cut into 1-inch pieces
2 teaspoons vegetable oil
¾ cup coarsely chopped onion
2 cloves garlic, minced
2 tablespoons teriyaki sauce
¼ cup diced deli ham
2 cups cooked vermicelli noodles

*Or substitute thawed frozen asparagus; omit step 1.

Chicken Fried Rice

1 bag SUCCESS® Rice
½ pound boneless skinless chicken, cut into ½-inch pieces
½ teaspoon salt
¼ teaspoon pepper
2 tablespoons vegetable oil
1 clove garlic, minced
½ teaspoon grated fresh ginger
2 cups diagonally sliced green onions
1 cup sliced fresh mushrooms
2 tablespoons reduced-sodium soy sauce
1 teaspoon sherry
1 teaspoon Asian-style hot chili sesame oil (optional)

Prepare rice according to package directions.

Sprinkle chicken with salt and pepper; set aside. Heat oil in large skillet over medium-high heat. Add garlic and ginger; cook and stir 1 minute. Add chicken; stir-fry until no longer pink in center. Add green onions and mushrooms; stir-fry until tender. Stir in soy sauce, sherry and sesame oil. Add rice; heat thoroughly, stirring occasionally.

Makes 6 servings

Skillet Chicken and Rice

1. Heat oil in 12-inch nonstick skillet over medium-high heat. Add chicken; cook 3 minutes on each side or until browned. Remove chicken from skillet.

2. Add onion, bell pepper, garlic and cumin seeds to skillet; cook and stir 5 minutes. Stir in tomatoes, chicken broth, rice, turkey-ham, salt and red pepper; bring to a boil.

3. Return chicken to skillet. Cover; reduce heat. Simmer 15 minutes. Turn chicken pieces over; place green beans over chicken. Cover; simmer 20 to 30 minutes or until chicken is no longer pink in center, rice and green beans are tender and all liquid is absorbed. Garnish as desired.

Makes 6 servings

1 teaspoon olive oil
2 boneless skinless chicken breasts, 2 skinless thighs, 2 skinless legs or any combination of 6 pieces (about 1½ pounds)
1 large onion, chopped
1 green bell pepper, seeded and chopped
1 clove garlic, minced
½ teaspoon cumin seeds
1 can (14 ounces) no-salt-added whole tomatoes, undrained
1½ cups fat-free reduced-sodium chicken broth
¾ cup uncooked rice
2 ounces (2 slices) turkey-ham, sliced into 2-inch pieces
¼ teaspoon salt
⅛ to ¼ teaspoon ground red pepper
8 ounces frozen cut green beans, thawed

Comforting Casseroles

Heartland Chicken Casserole

10 slices white bread, cubed
1½ cups cracker or dry
      bread crumbs, divided
4 cups cubed cooked
      chicken
3 cups chicken broth
1 cup chopped onion
1 cup chopped celery
1 can (8 ounces) sliced
      mushrooms, drained
1 jar (about 4 ounces)
      pimientos, diced
3 eggs, lightly beaten
      Salt and black pepper
1 tablespoon margarine

1. Preheat oven to 350°F.

2. Combine bread cubes and 1 cup cracker crumbs in large mixing bowl. Add chicken, broth, onion, celery, mushrooms, pimientos and eggs; mix well. Season with salt and pepper; spoon into 2½-quart casserole.

3. Melt margarine in small saucepan. Add remaining ½ cup cracker crumbs and brown, stirring occasionally. Sprinkle crumbs over casserole.

4. Bake 1 hour or until hot and bubbly.

Makes 6 servings

Chicken Enchilada Skillet Casserole

1 bag (16 ounces) **BIRDS EYE®** frozen Farm Fresh Mixtures Broccoli, Corn & Red Peppers

3 cups shredded cooked chicken

1 can (16 ounces) diced tomatoes, undrained

1 package (1¼ ounces) taco seasoning mix

1 cup shredded Monterey Jack cheese

8 ounces tortilla chips

• In large skillet, combine vegetables, chicken, tomatoes and seasoning mix; bring to boil over medium-high heat.

• Cover; cook 4 minutes or until vegetables are cooked and mixture is heated through.

• Sprinkle with cheese; cover and cook 2 minutes more or until cheese is melted.

• Serve with chips.   *Makes 4 servings*

Prep Time: *5 minutes*
Cook Time: *10 minutes*

Comforting Casseroles

Chicken-Asparagus Casserole

1. Preheat oven to 350°F. Grease 13×9-inch casserole; set aside.

2. Heat oil in small skillet over medium heat. Add bell peppers, onion and garlic; cook and stir until vegetables are crisp-tender.

3. Mix soup, ricotta cheese, 1 cup Cheddar cheese and eggs in large bowl until well blended. Add onion mixture, chicken, asparagus and noodles; mix well. Season with pepper, if desired.

4. Spread mixture evenly in prepared casserole. Top with remaining 1 cup Cheddar cheese.

5. Bake 30 minutes or until center is set and cheese is bubbly. Let stand 5 minutes before serving. Garnish as desired. *Makes 12 servings*

Tip: ½ pound fresh asparagus cut into ½-inch pieces can be substituted for frozen. Bring 6 cups water to a boil over high heat in large saucepan. Add fresh asparagus. Reduce heat to medium. Cover and cook 5 to 8 minutes or until crisp-tender. Drain.

2 teaspoons vegetable oil
1 cup seeded and chopped green and/or red bell peppers
1 medium onion, chopped
2 cloves garlic, minced
1 can (10¾ ounces) condensed cream of asparagus soup, undiluted
1 container (8 ounces) ricotta cheese
2 cups (8 ounces) shredded Cheddar cheese, divided
2 eggs
1½ cups chopped cooked chicken
1 package (10 ounces) frozen chopped asparagus, thawed and drained
8 ounces egg noodles, cooked
Black pepper (optional)

One-Crust Chicken Pot Pie

⅓ CRISCO® Butter Flavor
    Stick or ⅓ cup
    CRISCO® Butter Flavor
    Shortening
⅓ cup chopped onion
½ cup all-purpose
    baking mix
½ teaspoon salt
¼ teaspoon pepper
⅛ teaspoon thyme
1½ cups chicken broth
⅔ cup milk (add
    4 tablespoons PET®
    Evaporated Milk for
    a richer taste)
1½ cups frozen mixed
    vegetables
1¾ cups cooked chicken or
    turkey, chopped

Crust
2 cups all-purpose
    baking mix
4 tablespoons warm water
¼ CRISCO® Butter Flavor
    Stick or ¼ cup
    CRISCO® Butter Flavor
    Shortening

Preheat oven to 425°F. In a 2-quart saucepan, melt CRISCO® Shortening; add onion and cook until translucent. Add all-purpose baking mix. Add salt, pepper and thyme, stirring constantly. Add broth, then milk; bring to a slow, low boil. Add vegetables and chicken; keep over low heat while preparing crust.

For crust, mix all-purpose baking mix with water and CRISCO® Shortening. Pat out dough onto waxed paper; roll the crust to fit the dish you are using. The crust should be fairly thick. Carefully pour the filling into the baking dish. Fit the crust on top of the mixture; make slits for steam to escape. Bake for 25 to 30 minutes or until crust is lightly browned.   *Makes 4 to 6 servings*

Prep Time: *25 minutes*
Cook Time: *25 to 30 minutes*

Comforting Casseroles

Country Chicken and Biscuits

1. Preheat oven to 375°F.

2. Combine soup and milk in large bowl. Gently stir in chicken and green beans; season with pepper, if desired. Spoon into 11×7-inch or 2-quart microwavable dish.

3. Cover with plastic wrap; slit to vent. Microwave on HIGH 8 to 10 minutes or until heated through, rotating dish once. If using conventional oven, cover with foil and bake at 375°F, 20 to 25 minutes or until hot.

4. Separate biscuit dough into individual biscuits. Immediately arrange biscuits over hot mixture. Bake in conventional oven about 15 minutes or until biscuits are golden brown and baked through.   *Makes 4 servings*

1 can (10¾ ounces) condensed cream of celery soup
⅓ cup milk or water
4 boneless, skinless chicken breast halves, cooked and cut into bite-sized pieces
1 can (14½ ounces) DEL MONTE® Cut Green Beans, drained
1 can (11 ounces) refrigerated biscuits

Comforting Casseroles

Chicken Vera Cruz

1 chicken (3 pounds),
   cut up
1 jar (12 ounces) salsa
1⅓ cups *French's®* French
   Fried Onions, divided
½ cup Spanish stuffed
   olives, sliced
½ cup beer or nonalcoholic
   malt beverage
2 tablespoons lemon juice
2 tablespoons chopped
   fresh parsley *or*
   1 tablespoon dried
   parsley leaves
¼ teaspoon ground black
   pepper
   Cooked white rice
   (optional)

Preheat oven to 350°F. Place chicken in 2-quart shallow dish. Bake, uncovered, 40 minutes. Drain.

Combine salsa, ⅔ *cup* French Fried Onions, olives, beer, lemon juice, parsley and pepper in medium saucepan. Bring to a boil. Reduce heat to low. Cook and stir 5 minutes or until slightly thickened. Pour sauce over chicken. Bake 15 minutes or until chicken is no longer pink near bone. Sprinkle with remaining ⅔ *cup* onions. Bake 5 minutes or until onions are golden. Serve with rice, if desired.

Makes 4 to 6 servings

Prep Time: *15 minutes*
Cook Time: *60 minutes*

Comforting Casseroles

Apple Curry Chicken

1. Preheat oven to 350°F. Lightly grease 2-quart round baking dish.

2. Arrange chicken breasts in single layer in prepared dish.

3. Combine ¼ cup apple juice, salt and pepper in small bowl. Brush juice mixture over chicken.

4. Combine croutons, apple, onion, raisins, brown sugar, curry powder, poultry seasoning and garlic powder in large bowl. Toss with remaining ¾ cup apple juice.

5. Spread crouton mixture over chicken. Cover with foil; bake 45 minutes or until chicken is tender and no longer pink in center. Garnish as desired.

Makes 4 servings

4 boneless skinless chicken breasts
1 cup apple juice, divided
¼ teaspoon salt
 Dash black pepper
1½ cups plain croutons
1 medium apple, chopped
1 medium onion, chopped
¼ cup raisins
2 teaspoons brown sugar
1 teaspoon curry powder
¾ teaspoon poultry seasoning
⅛ teaspoon garlic powder
2 slices apple and fresh sprigs of thyme for garnish (optional)

Comforting Casseroles

Cheesy Chicken Enchiladas

¼ cup (½ stick) butter
1 cup chopped onion
2 cloves garlic, minced
¼ cup all-purpose flour
1 cup chicken broth
4 ounces cream cheese, softened
2 cups (8 ounces) shredded Mexican cheese blend, divided
1 cup shredded cooked chicken
1 can (7 ounces) chopped green chilies, drained
½ cup diced pimientos
6 (8-inch) flour tortillas, warmed
¼ cup chopped fresh cilantro
¾ cup prepared salsa

1. Preheat oven to 350°F. Spray 13×9-inch baking dish with nonstick cooking spray.

2. Melt butter in medium saucepan over medium heat. Add onion and garlic; cook and stir until onion is tender. Add flour; cook and stir 1 minute. Gradually whisk in chicken broth; cook and stir 2 to 3 minutes or until slightly thickened. Add cream cheese; stir until melted. Stir in ½ cup shredded cheese, chicken, chilies and pimientos.

3. Spoon about ⅓ cup mixture onto each tortilla. Roll up; place, seam side down, in prepared baking dish. Pour remaining mixture over enchiladas; sprinkle with remaining 1½ cups shredded cheese.

4. Bake 20 minutes or until bubbly and lightly browned. Sprinkle with cilantro and serve with salsa. *Makes 6 servings*

Classic Veg•All® Chicken Pot Pie

1. Preheat oven to 375°F. In medium bowl, combine Veg•All, chicken, soup, and thyme; mix well. Fit one pie crust into 9-inch pie pan; pour vegetable mixture into pie crust. Top with remaining crust; crimp edges to seal and prick top with fork.

2. Bake for 30 to 45 minutes (on lower rack) or until crust is golden brown and filling is hot. Allow pie to cool slightly before cutting into wedges to serve.

Makes 4 servings

2 cans (15 ounces each) VEG•ALL® Original Mixed Vegetables, drained

1 can (10 ounces) cooked chicken, drained

1 can (10¾ ounces) cream of chicken soup

¼ teaspoon thyme

¼ teaspoon pepper

2 (9-inch) frozen ready-to-bake pie crust

Cream of Chicken Soup

Dried Basil Leaves

Pie Crusts

Artichoke-Olive Chicken Bake

1½ cups uncooked rotini
1 tablespoon olive oil
1 medium onion, chopped
½ green bell pepper, chopped
2 cups shredded cooked chicken
1 can (14½ ounces) diced tomatoes with Italian-style herbs, undrained
1 can (14 ounces) artichoke hearts, drained and quartered
1 can (6 ounces) sliced black olives, drained
1 teaspoon dried Italian seasoning
2 cups (8 ounces) shredded mozzarella cheese

1. Preheat oven to 350°F. Spray 2-quart casserole with nonstick cooking spray.

2. Cook pasta according to package directions until al dente. Drain.

3. Heat oil in large deep skillet over medium heat until hot. Add onion and pepper; cook and stir 1 minute. Add pasta, chicken, tomatoes with juice, artichokes, olives and Italian seasoning; mix until blended.

4. Place half of chicken mixture in prepared dish; sprinkle with half of cheese. Top with remaining chicken mixture and cheese.

5. Bake, covered, 35 minutes or until hot and bubbly. *Makes 8 servings*

Comforting Casseroles

Chicken & Rice Bake

Preheat oven to 375°F. Combine soup, water, mushrooms, rice, ⅔ cup French Fried Onions and 2 teaspoons Worcestershire in 3-quart oblong baking dish. Arrange chicken over rice mixture. Brush chicken with remaining Worcestershire and sprinkle with paprika and thyme.

Bake, uncovered, 1 hour or until chicken is no longer pink in center. Top with remaining ⅔ cup onions. Bake 3 minutes or until onions are golden.

Makes 4 servings

Tip: Remove skin from chicken before baking, if desired.

Prep Time: *10 minutes*
Cook Time: *about 1 hour*

- 1 can (10¾ ounces) condensed cream of mushroom soup
- 1¾ cups water
- 1½ cups sliced mushrooms
- ¾ cup uncooked long-grain rice
- 1⅓ cups *French's®* French Fried Onions, divided
- 4 teaspoons *French's®* Worcestershire Sauce, divided
- 4 chicken breast halves (about 2 pounds)
- ½ teaspoon *each* paprika and dried thyme leaves

Bayou-Style Pot Pie

1 tablespoon olive oil
1 large onion, chopped
1 green bell pepper,
   chopped
1½ teaspoons minced garlic
½ pound boneless skinless
   chicken thighs, cut into
   1-inch pieces
1 can (14½ ounces) stewed
   tomatoes
½ pound fully cooked
   smoked sausage or
   kielbasa, thinly sliced
¾ teaspoon hot pepper
   sauce, or to taste
2¼ cups buttermilk baking
   mix
¾ teaspoon dried thyme
⅛ teaspoon black pepper
⅔ cup milk

1. Preheat oven to 450°F. Heat oil in medium ovenproof skillet over medium-high heat until hot. Add onion, bell pepper and garlic. Cook 3 minutes, stirring occasionally.

2. Add chicken and cook 1 minute. Add tomatoes, sausage and hot pepper sauce. Cook, uncovered, over medium-low heat 5 minutes.

3. While chicken is cooking, combine baking mix, thyme and black pepper. Stir in milk. Drop batter by heaping tablespoonfuls in mounds over chicken mixture. Bake 14 minutes or until biscuits are golden brown and cooked through and chicken mixture is bubbly. *Makes 4 servings*

Note: You can use any variety of fully cooked sausages from your supermarket meat case. Andouille, a fairly spicy Louisiana-style sausage, is perfect for this dish.

Prep and Cook Time: *28 minutes*

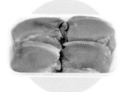

Spicy Chicken Casserole with Corn Bread

1. Preheat oven to 350°F. Spray 2-quart casserole with nonstick cooking spray. Set aside. Heat oil in large skillet over medium heat. Cook chicken until cooked through.

2. Sprinkle taco seasoning over chicken. Add black beans, tomatoes, corn, chilies and salsa; stir until well blended. Transfer to prepared dish.

3. Prepare corn bread mix according to package directions, adding cheese and bell pepper. Spread batter over chicken mixture.

4. Bake 30 minutes or until corn bread is golden brown.

Makes 4 to 6 servings

2 tablespoons olive oil
4 boneless skinless chicken breasts, cut into bite-size pieces
1 envelope (about 1 ounce) taco seasoning
1 can (about 15 ounces) black beans, rinsed and drained
1 can (14½ ounces) diced tomatoes, drained
1 can (about 10 ounces) Mexican-style corn, drained
1 can (about 4 ounces) diced green chilies, drained
½ cup mild salsa
1 box (about 8½ ounces) corn bread mix, plus ingredients to prepare
½ cup (2 ounces) shredded Cheddar cheese
¼ cup chopped red bell pepper

Comforting Casseroles

Chicken and Sweet Potato Ragoût

2 tablespoons vegetable oil, divided
1 (3-pound) chicken, cut into 8 pieces
1 large onion, chopped
1 (14½-ounce) can chicken broth
3 small sweet potatoes, peeled and cut into ¼-inch slices
2 cups shredded green cabbage
1 tablespoon TABASCO® brand Pepper Sauce
1 teaspoon salt
¼ cup water
1 tablespoon flour
¼ cup peanut butter

Heat 1 tablespoon oil in 12-inch skillet over medium heat. Add chicken; cook until well browned. Remove to plate. Add remaining 1 tablespoon oil and onion to skillet; cook 5 minutes. Return chicken to skillet; add broth, potatoes, cabbage, TABASCO® Sauce and salt. Heat to boiling over high heat. Reduce heat to low; cover and simmer 30 minutes or until tender, stirring occasionally.

Combine water and flour in small cup. Gradually stir into skillet with peanut butter. Cook over high heat until mixture thickens. *Makes 4 servings*

Comforting Casseroles

Chicken Normandy Style

1. Preheat oven to 350°F. Grease 9-inch square casserole dish.

2. Melt 1 tablespoon butter in 12-inch nonstick skillet. Add apple slices; cook and stir over medium heat 7 to 10 minutes or until tender. Remove apple slices from skillet.

3. Add ground chicken to same skillet; cook and stir over medium heat until brown, breaking up with spoon. Stir in apple brandy and cook 2 minutes. Stir in soup, green onions, sage, pepper and apple slices. Simmer 5 minutes.

4. Toss noodles with remaining 1 tablespoon butter. Spoon into prepared casserole. Top with chicken mixture. Bake 15 minutes or until hot.

Makes 4 servings

2 tablespoons butter, divided

3 cups peeled, thinly sliced apples, such as Fuji or Braeburn (about 3 apples)

1 pound ground chicken

¼ cup apple brandy or apple juice

1 can (10¾ ounces) condensed cream of chicken soup, undiluted

¼ cup finely chopped green onions (green part only)

2 teaspoons fresh minced sage *or* ½ teaspoon dried sage leaves

¼ teaspoon black pepper

1 package (12 ounces) egg noodles, cooked and drained

Cream of Chicken Soup

1 tablespoon butter
1 tablespoon olive oil
2 boneless skinless
    chicken breasts
    (about ½ pound), cut
    into bite-size pieces
2 cloves garlic, minced
1 cup sliced mushrooms
2 cups sliced asparagus
    Black pepper
1 package (about 6 ounces)
    corn bread stuffing mix
¼ cup dry white wine
1 can (14½ ounces)
    chicken broth
1 can (10½ ounces)
    condensed cream of
    asparagus soup,
    undiluted

Comforting Casseroles

Chicken, Asparagus & Mushroom Bake

1. Preheat oven to 350°F. Heat butter and oil in large skillet until butter is melted. Cook and stir chicken and garlic about 3 minutes over medium-high heat until chicken is cooked through. Add mushrooms; cook and stir 2 minutes. Add asparagus; cook and stir about 5 minutes or until asparagus is crisp-tender. Season with pepper.

2. Transfer mixture to 2½-quart casserole or 6 small casseroles. Top with stuffing mix.

3. Add wine to skillet; cook and stir 1 minute over medium-high heat, scraping up any browned bits from bottom of skillet. Add broth and soup; cook and stir until well blended.

4. Pour broth mixture into casserole; mix well. Bake, uncovered, about 35 minutes (30 minutes for small casseroles) or until heated through and lightly browned.   *Makes 6 servings*

Creole Chicken Thighs & Rice

1. Heat oil in large skillet or Dutch oven over medium heat until hot. Sprinkle chicken with salt, paprika, thyme and black pepper. Cook chicken 5 to 6 minutes on each side or until golden brown. Remove from skillet.

2. Add onion, celery, bell pepper and garlic to same skillet; cook 2 minutes. Add rice; cook 2 minutes, stirring to coat rice with oil. Stir in tomatoes with juice, water. Season to taste with hot pepper sauce; bring to a boil.

3. Arrange chicken over rice mixture; reduce heat. Cover; simmer 20 minutes or until chicken is no longer pink in center and liquid is absorbed.

Makes 4 servings

2 tablespoons vegetable oil
2¼ pounds chicken thighs
½ teaspoon salt
½ teaspoon paprika
½ teaspoon dried thyme
¼ teaspoon black pepper
½ cup chopped onion
½ cup chopped celery
½ cup chopped green bell pepper
2 cloves garlic, minced
1 cup long grain or converted rice
1 can (14½ ounces) diced tomatoes, undrained
1 cup water
Hot pepper sauce

Paprika

LONG GRAIN RICE

Diced Tomatoes

Comforting Casseroles

Great Grilling

Thai Grilled Chicken

4 boneless chicken breasts, skinned if desired (about 1¼ pounds)
¼ cup soy sauce
2 teaspoons bottled minced garlic
½ teaspoon red pepper flakes
2 tablespoons honey
1 tablespoon fresh lime juice

1. Prepare grill for direct cooking. Place chicken in shallow baking dish. Combine soy sauce, garlic and pepper flakes in measuring cup. Pour over chicken, turning to coat. Let stand 10 minutes.

2. Meanwhile, combine honey and lime juice in small bowl until blended; set aside.

3. Place chicken on grid over medium coals; brush with marinade. Discard remaining marinade. Grill, covered, 5 minutes. Brush both sides of chicken with honey mixture. Grill 5 minutes more or until chicken is no longer pink in center. *Makes 4 servings*

Serving suggestion: Serve with steamed white rice, Oriental vegetables and fresh fruit salad.

Prep and Cook Time: *25 minutes*

Grilled Marinated Chicken

8 whole chicken legs
(thighs and drumsticks
attached) (about
3½ pounds)
6 ounces frozen lemonade
concentrate, thawed
2 tablespoons white wine
vinegar
1 tablespoon grated lemon
peel
2 cloves garlic, minced

1. Remove skin and all visible fat from chicken. Place chicken in 13×9-inch glass baking dish. Combine remaining ingredients in small bowl; blend well. Pour over chicken; turn to coat. Cover; refrigerate 3 hours or overnight, turning occasionally.

2. To prevent sticking, spray grid with nonstick cooking spray. Prepare coals for grilling.

3. Place chicken on grill 4 inches from medium-hot coals. Grill 20 to 30 minutes or until chicken is no longer pink near bone, turning occasionally. Garnish with curly endive and lemon peel strips, if desired.

Makes 8 servings

Herb Garlic Grilled Chicken

Combine parsley, garlic, lemon peel and mint. Loosen skin from breast and thigh portions of chicken quarters by running fingers between skin and meat. Rub some of seasoning mixture evenly over meat under skin, replace skin and rub remaining seasonings over outside of chicken to cover evenly. Arrange medium-hot KINGSFORD® Briquets on one side of covered grill. Place chicken on grid opposite coals. Cover grill and cook chicken 45 to 55 minutes, turning once or twice. Chicken is done when juices run clear.

Makes 4 servings

¼ cup chopped parsley
1½ tablespoons minced garlic
4 teaspoons grated lemon peel
1 tablespoon chopped fresh mint
1 chicken (2½ to 3 pounds), quartered

Grilled Rosemary Chicken

2 tablespoons lemon juice
2 tablespoons olive oil
2 tablespoons minced fresh
   rosemary
2 cloves garlic, minced
¼ teaspoon salt
4 boneless skinless chicken
   breasts (about 1 pound)

1. Spray cold grid of grill with nonstick cooking spray. Prepare grill for direct grilling.

2. Whisk together lemon juice, oil, rosemary, garlic and salt in small bowl. Pour into shallow glass dish. Add chicken, turning to coat both sides with lemon juice mixture. Cover; marinate in refrigerator 15 minutes, turning chicken once. Remove chicken; discard marinade.

3. Grill chicken over medium-hot coals 5 to 6 minutes per side or until chicken is no longer pink in center. Serve with grilled or steamed fresh vegetables; if desired. *Makes 4 servings*

Cook's Note: For added flavor, moisten a few sprigs of fresh rosemary and toss on the hot coals just before grilling.

Prep and Cook Time: *30 minutes*

Persian Chicken Breasts

1. Remove lemon peel in long strips with paring knife; reserve for garnish. Juice lemon; combine juice with oil, cinnamon, salt, pepper and turmeric in large heavy-duty resealable plastic food storage bag. Gently knead ingredients in bag to mix thoroughly; add chicken. Seal bag and turn to coat thoroughly. Refrigerate 4 hours or overnight.

2. Remove chicken from marinade; gently shake to remove excess. Discard remaining marinade. Grill chicken 5 to 7 minutes per side or until chicken is no longer pink in center. Serve chicken with lightly grilled tortillas and grilled vegetables, if desired. *Makes 4 servings*

1 medium lemon
2 teaspoons olive oil
1 teaspoon ground cinnamon
½ teaspoon salt
¼ teaspoon black pepper
¼ teaspoon turmeric
4 boneless skinless chicken breasts
4 flour tortillas or soft lavash (optional)
Grilled vegetables (optional)

Grilled Ginger Chicken with Pineapple and Coconut Rice

1 can (20 ounces)
    pineapple slices in
    juice
⅔ cup uncooked white rice
½ cup unsweetened flaked
    coconut
4 boneless skinless chicken
    breasts (about 1 pound)
1 tablespoon soy sauce
1 teaspoon ground ginger

1. Drain juice from pineapple into glass measure. Reserve 2 tablespoons juice. Combine remaining juice with enough water to equal 2 cups.

2. Cook and stir rice and coconut in medium saucepan over medium heat 3 to 4 minutes or until lightly browned. Add juice mixture; cover and bring to a boil. Reduce heat to low; cook 15 minutes or until rice is tender and liquid is absorbed.

3. While rice is cooking, combine chicken, reserved 2 tablespoons juice, soy sauce and ginger in medium bowl; toss well.

4. Grill or broil chicken 6 minutes; turn. Add pineapple to grill or broiler pan. Cook 6 to 8 minutes or until chicken is no longer pink in center, turning pineapple after 3 minutes.

5. Transfer rice to four serving plates; serve with chicken and pineapple.

Makes 4 servings

Prep and Cook Time: *22 minutes*

57 & Honey Glazed Kabobs

Combine 57 Sauce and honey; set aside. Alternately thread chicken and vegetables on skewers. Spray with cooking spray. Grill over medium heat 12 to 15 minutes, turning often, until chicken is cooked. Brush liberally with 57 Sauce mixture. Grill until kabobs are brown and glazed, about 5 minutes.

Makes 4 servings

⅔ cup **HEINZ 57 Sauce**®
⅓ cup **honey**
4 **skinless boneless chicken breast halves, each cut into 8 cubes (about 1 pound)**
Fresh vegetables, cut into 1½ inch pieces (such as onions, mushrooms, bell peppers, zucchini and yellow squash)
Cooking spray

Grilled Chicken, Rice & Veggies

1 boneless skinless chicken breast (about 3 ounces)

3 tablespoons reduced-fat Italian salad dressing, divided

½ cup fat-free reduced-sodium chicken broth

¼ cup uncooked rice

½ cup frozen broccoli and carrot blend, thawed

1. Place chicken and 1 tablespoon salad dressing in resealable plastic food storage bag. Seal bag; turn to coat. Marinate in refrigerator 1 hour.

2. Remove chicken from marinade; discard marinade. Grill chicken over medium-hot coals 8 to 10 minutes or until chicken is no longer pink in center.

3. Meanwhile, bring broth to a boil in small saucepan; add rice. Cover; reduce heat and simmer 15 minutes, stirring in vegetables during last 5 minutes of cooking. Remove from heat and stir in remaining 2 tablespoons dressing. Serve with chicken.

Makes 1 serving

Chicken Thighs with Ginger-Lime Marinade

For marinade, combine all ingredients except chicken. In large, shallow nonaluminum baking dish or plastic bag, pour ¾ cup marinade over chicken; turn to coat. Cover, or close bag, and marinate in refrigerator, turning occasionally, 3 to 24 hours. Refrigerate remaining marinade.

Remove chicken from marinade, discarding marinade. Grill or broil chicken, turning once and brushing frequently with refrigerated marinade, 12 minutes or until chicken is thoroughly cooked. *Makes 4 servings*

¾ cup **WISH-BONE®** Italian
 Dressing*
2½ tablespoons honey
 4 teaspoons lime juice
 1 teaspoon ground ginger
¼ teaspoon crushed red
 pepper flakes
 (optional)
 6 medium chicken thighs
 (about 2 pounds)

*Also terrific with WISH-BONE® Robusto Italian Dressing.

Grilled Chicken Breasts with Zesty Peanut Sauce

8 large boneless, skinless chicken breast halves

Marinade
½ cup soy sauce
⅓ cup fresh lime juice
¼ cup CRISCO® All-Vegetable Oil
2 tablespoons JIF® Creamy or Extra Crunchy Peanut Butter
1 tablespoon brown sugar
2 large cloves garlic, minced
½ teaspoon salt
½ teaspoon cayenne pepper

Sauce
1 cup JIF® Creamy or Extra Crunchy Peanut Butter
1 cup unsweetened coconut milk
¼ cup fresh lime juice
3 tablespoons soy sauce
2 tablespoons dark brown sugar
2 teaspoons minced fresh ginger root
2 cloves garlic, minced
¼ teaspoon cayenne pepper, or to taste
½ cup chicken stock
½ cup heavy cream
Chopped fresh cilantro for garnish

Wash, trim and pound the chicken to ¼-inch thickness.

Combine chicken and next 8 ingredients in a plastic bag. Marinate 1 hour or overnight in the refrigerator.

Combine next 8 ingredients in a saucepan over medium heat. Cook 15 minutes, stirring constantly. Whisk in stock and cream. Cook 1 minute. Set aside.

Preheat grill. Remove chicken from marinade and place on a hot grid. Grill 4 to 6 minutes on each side or until center is no longer pink. Serve hot topped with the peanut sauce. Sprinkle with cilantro.   *Makes 8 servings*

Spicy Island Chicken

1. Combine all ingredients except chicken in medium bowl; mix well. Place chicken in resealable plastic food storage bag and add seasoning mixture. Seal bag; turn to coat chicken. Marinate in refrigerator 4 hours or overnight.

2. Spray cold grid with nonstick cooking spray. Adjust grid to 4 to 6 inches above heat. Preheat grill to medium-high heat.

3. Remove chicken from marinade. Grill 5 to 7 minutes per side or until chicken is no longer pink in center, brushing occasionally with marinade. *Do not brush with marinade during last 5 minutes of grilling.* Discard remaining marinade. Serve with grilled sweet potatoes. Garnish, if desired.

Makes 6 servings

- 1 cup finely chopped onion
- ⅓ cup white wine vinegar
- 6 green onions, finely chopped
- 6 cloves garlic, minced
- 1 habañero or serrano pepper,* finely chopped
- 4½ teaspoons olive oil
- 4½ teaspoons fresh thyme leaves *or* 2 teaspoons dried thyme leaves
- 1 tablespoon ground allspice
- 2 teaspoons sugar
- 1 teaspoon salt
- 1 teaspoon ground cinnamon
- 1 teaspoon ground nutmeg
- 1 teaspoon black pepper
- ½ teaspoon ground red pepper
- 6 boneless skinless chicken breasts

Habañero peppers can sting and irritate the skin; wear rubber gloves when handling peppers and do not touch eyes. Wash hands after handling.

Blue Cheese Stuffed Chicken Breasts

½ cup (2 ounces) crumbled
    blue cheese
2 tablespoons **margarine** or
    butter, softened,
    divided
¾ teaspoon **dried thyme**
    leaves
4 boneless **chicken breasts**
    with skin
1 tablespoon **lemon juice**
½ teaspoon **paprika**

1. Prepare grid for grilling. Combine blue cheese, 1 tablespoon margarine and thyme in small bowl until blended. Season with salt and pepper.

2. Loosen skin over breast of chicken by pushing fingers between skin and meat, taking care not to tear skin. Spread blue cheese mixture under skin with rubber spatula or small spoon; massage skin to evenly spread cheese mixture.

3. Place chicken, skin side down, on grid over medium coals. Grill, covered, 5 minutes. Meanwhile, melt remaining 1 tablespoon margarine; stir in lemon juice and paprika. Turn chicken; brush with lemon juice mixture. Grill 5 to 7 minutes more or until chicken is no longer pink in center. Transfer chicken to carving board; cut each breast in half. *Makes 4 servings*

Serving Suggestion: Serve with steamed new potatoes and broccoli.

Prep and Cook Time: *22 minutes*

Great Grilling

Grilled Chicken and Vegetable Kabobs

1. Combine oil, lemon juice, garlic, salt, lemon pepper and tarragon in large resealable plastic food storage bag. Add chicken, mushrooms, zucchini, bell peppers, onion and tomatoes. Seal and shake until well coated. Refrigerate at least 8 hours, turning occasionally.

2. Soak 6 (10-inch) wooden skewers in water 30 minutes; set aside.

3. Remove chicken and vegetables from marinade; discard marinade. Thread chicken and vegetables onto skewers.

4. Coat grill grid with nonstick cooking spray; place skewers on grid. Grill, covered, over medium-hot coals 3 to 4 minutes on each side or until chicken is no longer pink in center.

5. Remove chicken and vegetables from skewers and serve over rice.

Makes 6 servings

Serving Suggestion: Serve with sliced fresh pineapple and green grapes.

⅓ cup olive oil
¼ cup lemon juice
4 cloves garlic, coarsely chopped
½ teaspoon salt
½ teaspoon lemon pepper
½ teaspoon dried tarragon leaves
1 pound chicken tenders
6 ounces mushrooms
1 cup sliced zucchini
½ cup cubed green bell pepper
½ cup cubed red bell pepper
1 red onion, quartered
6 cherry tomatoes
3 cups hot cooked rice

Lime-Mustard Marinated Chicken

2 boneless skinless chicken breasts (about 3 ounces each)
¼ cup fresh lime juice
3 tablespoons honey mustard, divided
2 teaspoons olive oil
¼ teaspoon ground cumin
⅛ teaspoon garlic powder
⅛ teaspoon ground red pepper
¾ cup plus 2 tablespoons fat-free, reduced-sodium chicken broth, divided
¼ cup uncooked rice
1 cup broccoli florets
⅓ cup matchstick carrots

1. Rinse chicken. Pat dry with paper towels. Place in resealable plastic food storage bag. Whisk together lime juice, 2 tablespoons mustard, olive oil, cumin, garlic powder and red pepper. Pour over chicken. Seal bag. Marinate in refrigerator 2 hours.

2. Combine ¾ cup chicken broth, rice and remaining 1 tablespoon mustard in small saucepan. Bring to a boil. Reduce heat and simmer, covered, 12 minutes or until rice is almost tender. Stir in broccoli, carrots and remaining 2 tablespoons chicken broth. Cook, covered, 2 to 3 minutes more or until vegetables are crisp-tender and rice is tender.

3. Meanwhile, drain chicken, discard marinade. Prepare grill for direct grilling. Grill chicken over medium coals 10 to 13 minutes or until no longer pink in center. Serve chicken with rice mixture. *Makes 2 servings*

Great Grilling

Grilled Chicken with Spicy Black Beans & Rice

1. Spray cold grid of grill with nonstick cooking spray. Prepare grill for direct grilling. Rub chicken with jerk seasoning. Grill over medium-hot coals 8 to 10 minutes or until no longer pink in center.

2. Meanwhile, heat oil in medium saucepan or skillet over medium heat. Add bell pepper and chili powder; cook and stir until peppers are soft.

3. Add rice, beans, pimiento and olives to saucepan. Cook about 3 minutes or until hot.

4. Serve bean mixture with chicken. Top bean mixture with onion. Garnish as desired.

Makes 2 servings

1 boneless skinless chicken breast (about ¼ pound)
½ teaspoon Caribbean jerk seasoning
½ teaspoon olive oil
¼ cup finely diced green bell pepper
2 teaspoons chipotle chili powder
¾ cup hot cooked rice
½ cup rinsed and drained canned black beans
2 tablespoons diced pimiento
1 tablespoon chopped pimiento-stuffed green olives
1 tablespoon chopped onion

Citrus Marinated Chicken

1 cup orange juice
¼ cup lemon juice
¼ cup lime juice
2 cloves garlic, pressed or minced
4 boneless skinless chicken breast halves
Salt and black pepper
Citrus Tarragon Butter (recipe follows)
Hot cooked couscous with green onion slices and slivered almonds (optional)
Lemon and lime slices and Italian parsley for garnish

Combine orange, lemon and lime juices and garlic in a shallow glass dish or large heavy plastic bag. Add chicken; cover dish or close bag. Marinate in refrigerator no more than 2 hours. (Lemon and lime juice will "cook" the chicken if it's left in too long.) Remove chicken from marinade; discard marinade. Season chicken with salt and pepper.

Oil hot grid to help prevent sticking. Grill chicken, on a covered grill, over medium KINGSFORD® Briquets, 6 to 8 minutes until chicken is cooked through, turning once. Serve topped with a dollop of Citrus Tarragon Butter. Serve over couscous, if desired. Garnish, if desired.   *Makes 4 servings*

Citrus Tarragon Butter

½ cup butter, softened
1 tablespoon finely chopped fresh tarragon
1 tablespoon orange juice
1 teaspoon finely grated orange peel
1 teaspoon finely grated lemon peel

Beat butter in a small bowl until soft and light. Stir in remaining ingredients. Cover and refrigerate until ready to serve.   *Makes about ½ cup*

Grilled Chicken Breasts with Tropical Salsa

Grill chicken fillets 4 to 5 minutes on each side or until internal temperature reaches 170°F and no longer pink in center. Combine mango, kiwi, onions, cilantro, lime juice and red pepper flakes in medium bowl. Serve with chicken.   *Makes 4 servings*

Prep Time: *20 minutes*

1 package BUTTERBALL®
  Skinless Boneless
  Chicken Breast Fillets
1 cup cubed mango
1 kiwi, diced
2 green onions, chopped
2 tablespoons chopped
  fresh cilantro
1 tablespoon fresh lime
  juice
½ teaspoon red pepper
  flakes

Grilled Lemon Chicken Dijon

⅓ cup HOLLAND HOUSE®
White with Lemon
Cooking Wine

⅓ cup olive oil

2 tablespoons Dijon
mustard

1 teaspoon dried thyme
leaves

2 whole chicken breasts,
skinned, boned and
halved

In shallow baking dish combine cooking wine, oil, mustard and thyme. Add chicken and turn to coat. Cover; marinate in refrigerator for 1 to 2 hours.

Prepare grill for direct cooking. Drain chicken, reserving marinade. Grill chicken over medium coals 12 to 16 minutes or until cooked through, turning once and basting with marinade.*

Makes 4 servings

Do not baste during last 5 minutes of grilling.

Grilled Garlic Chicken

1. In medium bowl, combine soup mix with oil.
2. Add chicken; toss to coat.
3. Grill or broil until chicken is thoroughly cooked. *Makes 4 servings*

**1 envelope LIPTON®
RECIPE SECRETS®
Savory Herb with
Garlic Soup Mix**
**3 tablespoons BERTOLLI®
Olive Oil**
**4 boneless, skinless
chicken breast halves
(about 1¼ pounds)**

Weeknight Meals

Roast Garlic Chicken

1 whole broiler-fryer
    chicken (about 3 to
    4 pounds)
2 tablespoons lemon juice
1½ teaspoons LAWRY'S®
    Garlic Powder With
    Parsley
2 teaspoons LAWRY'S®
    Seasoned Salt

Sprinkle chicken with lemon juice, Garlic Powder With Parsley and Seasoned Salt over outside and inside cavity of chicken. Spray 13×9×2-inch baking dish and roasting rack with nonstick cooking spray. Place chicken, breast side up, on roasting rack. Roast in 400°F oven 70 minutes, or until chicken is thoroughly cooked. Let stand 10 minutes before carving.

Makes 6 servings

Hint: Loosely 'crunch up' some foil in the dish around the chicken to keep grease from splattering in the oven.

Prep Time: *10 minutes*
Cook Time: *70 minutes*

Hidden Valley® Fried Chicken

1 broiler-fryer chicken,
cut up (2 to 2½ pounds)
1 cup prepared HIDDEN
VALLEY® The Original
Ranch® Dressing
¾ cup all-purpose flour
1 teaspoon salt
½ teaspoon freshly ground
black pepper
Vegetable oil

Place chicken pieces in shallow baking dish; pour salad dressing over chicken. Cover; refrigerate at least 8 hours. Remove chicken. Shake off excess marinade; discard marinade. Preheat oven to 350°F. On plate, mix flour, salt and pepper; roll chicken in seasoned flour. Heat ½ inch oil in large skillet until small cube of bread dropped into oil browns in 60 seconds or until oil is 375°F. Fry chicken until golden, 5 to 7 minutes on each side; transfer to baking pan. Bake until chicken is tender and juices run clear, about 30 minutes. Serve with corn muffins, if desired.

Makes 4 main-dish servings

San Marino Chicken

Slow Cooker Directions

1. Lightly coat chicken pieces with flour. Place chicken in slow cooker. Add tomato sauce, sun-dried tomatoes, wine and lemon peel. Cover and cook on LOW setting for 4 hours (or on HIGH for 2 hours).

2. Add mushrooms and *1 cup* French Fried Onions. Cover and cook on LOW setting for 2 hours (or on HIGH for 1 hour) until chicken is no longer pink near bone. Remove chicken to heated platter. Skim fat from sauce.

3. Serve chicken with hot cooked rice or pasta, if desired. Spoon sauce on top and sprinkle with remaining onions.   *Makes 4 servings*

Prep Time: *5 minutes*
Cook Time: *6 hours*

1 chicken (3 pounds), skinned and cut up
¼ cup all-purpose flour
1 can (8 ounces) tomato sauce
⅓ cup chopped sun-dried tomatoes packed in oil
¼ cup red wine
1 tablespoon grated lemon peel
2 cups sliced mushrooms
2 cups *French's®* French Fried Onions, divided
Hot cooked rice or pasta (optional)

Country Roasted Chicken Dinner

1 envelope LIPTON®
    RECIPE SECRETS®
    Savory Herb with
    Garlic Soup Mix*

2 tablespoons honey

1 tablespoon water

1 tablespoon I CAN'T
    BELIEVE IT'S NOT
    BUTTER!® Spread,
    melted

1 roasting chicken
    (5 to 6 pounds)

3 pounds all-purpose
    and/or sweet potatoes,
    cut into chunks

*Also terrific with Lipton® Recipe Secrets® Golden Herb with Lemon or Golden Onion Soup Mix.

Preheat oven to 350°F.

In small bowl, blend savory herb with garlic soup mix, honey, water and I Can't Believe It's Not Butter!® Spread.

In 18×12-inch roasting pan, arrange chicken, breast side up; brush with soup mixture. Cover loosely with aluminum foil. Roast 30 minutes; drain off drippings. Arrange potatoes around chicken and continue roasting covered, stirring potatoes occasionally, 1 hour or until meat thermometer reaches 175°F and potatoes are tender. *If chicken reaches 175°F before potatoes are tender, remove chicken to serving platter and keep warm. Continue roasting potatoes until tender.*   *Makes about 8 servings*

Note: Insert meat thermometer into thickest part of thigh between breast and thigh. Make sure tip does not touch bone.

Serving Suggestion: Serve with a mixed green salad, warm biscuits and Lipton® Iced Tea.

Chicken and Pasta Primavera

• In large skillet, melt I Can't Believe It's Not Butter!® Spread over medium-high heat and cook chicken and garlic, stirring frequently, 5 minutes.

• Stir in water, wine, recipe mix and pepper. Bring to a boil over high heat, stirring constantly. Reduce heat to low and simmer 5 minutes or until chicken is thoroughly cooked.

• Toss chicken mixture with hot linguine. Serve, if desired, with grated cheese.   *Makes 6 servings*

Prep Time: *20 minutes*
Cook Time: *12 minutes*

1 tablespoon I CAN'T BELIEVE IT'S NOT BUTTER!® Spread
¾ pound boneless, skinless chicken breasts, cut into thin strips
2 cloves garlic, finely chopped
1 cup water
½ cup dry white wine or water
1 package KNORR® Recipe Classics™ Spring Vegetable Soup, Dip and Recipe Mix
½ teaspoon freshly ground pepper
8 ounces linguine, cooked and drained
  Grated Parmesan cheese (optional)

Blackened Santa Fe Chicken

1½ cups *French's*® French Fried Onions, divided

¼ cup chopped fresh cilantro

1 tablespoon chili powder

2 teaspoons ground cumin

½ teaspoon salt

4 boneless skinless chicken breast halves

1 egg, beaten

1 cup (4 ounces) shredded taco blend cheese

1 cup mild salsa

Garnish: cilantro sprigs (optional)

1. Finely crush *1 cup* French Fried Onions. Place in pie plate; stir in cilantro, chili powder, cumin and salt. Reserve remaining onions.

2. Dip chicken into beaten egg, then into crumb mixture, pressing gently to coat lightly.

3. Heat 2 tablespoons oil in nonstick skillet over medium-high heat. Add chicken and sauté 10 minutes or until chicken is no longer pink in center, turning once. Sprinkle with cheese and remaining onions. Cook, covered, until cheese melts. Serve with salsa and garnish with cilantro sprigs, if desired.

Makes 4 servings

Variation: For added Cheddar flavor, substitute *French's*® **Cheddar French Fried Onions** for the original flavor.

Prep Time: *15 minutes*
Cook Time: *12 minutes*

Tropical Chicken Salad Pockets

In bowl, place chicken, pineapple, green onions, and cilantro. Pour dressing over chicken mixture and toss to mix. Line each pocket bread with lettuce leaf; fill with chicken salad. *Makes 4 servings*

Tropical Dressing: In small bowl, mix together ½ cup reduced-fat mayonnaise, 1 tablespoon lime juice, 1 tablespoon reserved pineapple juice, 1 teaspoon sugar, 1 teaspoon curry powder, ½ teaspoon salt, and ¼ teaspoon grated lime peel. Makes about ⅔ cup dressing.

Favorite recipe from **Delmarva Poultry Industry, Inc.**

3 cups diced cooked chicken*
1 can (20 ounces) pineapple chunks in juice, drained, juice reserved
3 green onions, thinly sliced
2 tablespoons chopped fresh cilantro
  Tropical Dressing (recipe follows)
4 pocket breads, slit
  Lettuce leaves

Use home-roasted chicken, or ready-to-eat roasted chicken from the supermarket or deli.

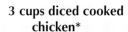

Herbed Chicken and Vegetables

¾ teaspoon dried oregano
    leaves, divided
1 teaspoon paprika
¼ teaspoon salt
⅛ teaspoon black pepper
2 skinless bone-in chicken
    breasts
2 sheets (18×12 inches
    each) heavy-duty foil,
    lightly sprayed with
    nonstick cooking spray
½ cup pasta sauce
4 cloves garlic, minced
½ medium green bell
    pepper, cut into squares
½ medium yellow bell
    pepper, cut into squares
½ cup chopped fresh
    mushrooms
¼ cup chopped onion
    Parmesan cheese

1. Preheat toaster oven or oven to 450°F. In small bowl, combine ½ teaspoon oregano, paprika, salt and pepper; mix well.

2. Place chicken on foil sheets. Sprinkle each chicken breast with half of oregano mixture. Combine pasta sauce, garlic, bell peppers, mushrooms, onion and remaining ¼ teaspoon oregano in medium bowl. Pour half of sauce mixture over each chicken breast.

3. Double foil sides and ends of foil to seal packets, leaving head space for heat circulation. Place packets on toaster oven tray (or baking sheet if using oven).

4. Bake 23 to 25 minutes or until chicken juices run clear. Carefully open ends of packets to allow steam to escape. Open packets and transfer contents to serving plates. Sprinkle with Parmesan cheese. Serve with noodles.

Makes 2 servings

Serving Suggestion: For a hearty meal, serve this dish with hot cooked egg noodles.

Weeknight Meals

Yummy Weeknight Chicken

1. Heat *1 tablespoon oil* in large nonstick skillet over medium-high heat. Cook chicken 5 minutes until chicken is no longer pink in center. Remove chicken to serving platter; keep warm.

2. In same skillet, sauté onion and mushrooms for 5 minutes or until mushrooms are golden brown and no liquid remains. Return chicken to skillet.

3. Combine remaining ingredients. Pour into skillet. Bring to a full boil. Reduce heat and cook 2 to 3 minutes or until sauce thickens slightly, stirring occasionally. Serve with hot cooked rice, if desired.   *Makes 4 servings*

Prep Time: *10 minutes*
Cook Time: *12 minutes*

**1 pound boneless skinless
    chicken breasts,
    pounded thin
1 small onion, sliced
1 package (10 ounces)
    mushrooms, sliced
⅓ cup barbecue sauce
¼ cup honey
2 tablespoons *French's*®
    Worcestershire Sauce**

Quick Chicken Jambalaya

8 boneless, skinless
     chicken thighs,
     cut in bite-size pieces
¼ teaspoon garlic salt
1 tablespoon vegetable oil
2½ cups 8-vegetable juice
1 bag (16 ounces) frozen
     pepper stir-fry mix
½ cup diced cooked ham
1 teaspoon hot pepper
     sauce
1¾ cups quick cooking rice,
     uncooked

Sprinkle garlic salt over chicken. In large nonstick skillet, place oil and heat to medium-high temperature. Add chicken and cook, stirring occasionally, 8 minutes or until chicken is lightly browned. Add vegetable juice, pepper stir-fry mix, ham, and hot pepper sauce. Heat to boiling; cover and cook over medium heat 4 minutes. Stir in rice; heat to boiling. Cover, remove pan from heat and let stand 5 minutes or until rice and vegetables are tender and liquid is absorbed.   *Makes 4 servings*

Favorite recipe from **Delmarva Poultry Industry, Inc.**

Weeknight Meals

Roast Chicken with Peppers

1. Preheat oven to 375°F. Rinse chicken in cold water; pat dry with paper towels. Place in shallow roasting pan.

2. Combine 2 tablespoons oil, rosemary and lemon juice; brush over chicken. Sprinkle 1 teaspoon salt and ½ teaspoon pepper over chicken. Roast 15 minutes.

3. Cut bell peppers lengthwise into ½-inch-thick strips. Cut onion into thin wedges. Toss vegetables with remaining 1 tablespoon oil, ¼ teaspoon salt and ¼ teaspoon pepper. Spoon vegetables around chicken; roast about 4 minutes or until vegetables are tender and chicken is no longer pink and juices run clear. Serve chicken with vegetables and pan juices.   *Makes 6 servings*

1 chicken (3 to 3½ pounds), cut into pieces

3 tablespoons olive oil, divided

1 tablespoon plus 1½ teaspoons chopped fresh rosemary *or* 1½ teaspoons dried rosemary

1 tablespoon fresh lemon juice

1¼ teaspoons salt, divided

¾ teaspoon freshly ground black pepper, divided

3 bell peppers (preferably 1 red, 1 yellow and 1 green)

1 medium onion

Hot & Sour Chicken

4 to 6 boneless skinless
   chicken breasts
   (about 1 to 1½ pounds)
1 package (1 ounce) dry
   hot-and-sour soup mix
1 cup chicken or vegetable
   broth

Slow Cooker Directions

Place chicken in slow cooker. Add soup mix and broth. Cover; cook on LOW 5 to 6 hours. Garnish as desired. *Makes 4 to 6 servings*

Serving Suggestions: This dish can be served over steamed white rice and topped with crispy Chinese noodles. Or, for a colorful variation, serve it over a bed of snow peas and sugar snap peas tossed with diced red bell pepper.

Creamy Chicken and Linguine

Cook linguine according to package directions; drain.

In a large skillet, heat CRISCO® Oil over medium heat. Add chicken, onion, garlic, and mushrooms; sauté until onions are soft and chicken is lightly browned. Stir in salt, pepper, and cayenne pepper. Add green onions, diced tomatoes with juice and PET® Evaporated Milk; bring to a boil, reduce heat and stir. Simmer 5 to 6 minutes. Toss with pasta; serve.

Makes 4 to 6 servings

Prep time: *10 minutes*
Cook time: *15 minutes*

8 ounces linguine
¼ cup CRISCO® Canola Oil*
2 boneless chicken breast halves, cut into bite-size pieces
1 onion, finely chopped
2 cloves garlic, minced
8 ounces button mushrooms, sliced
½ teaspoon salt
⅛ teaspoon black pepper
⅛ teaspoon cayenne pepper
3 green onions, thinly sliced
1 15-ounce can diced tomatoes
1 5-ounce can PET® Evaporated Milk

*Or use your favorite CRISCO® Oil

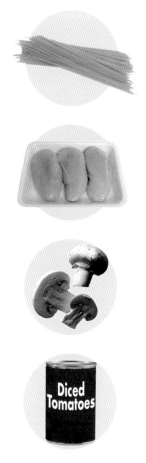

Weeknight Meals

Spicy Buttermilk-Battered Fried Chicken

2 cups buttermilk
3 teaspoons red pepper sauce
1 3 to 4 pound chicken cut into 8 pieces, rinsed and patted dry
2½ cups PILLSBURY BEST® All-Purpose or Unbleached Flour
1 tablespoon dried oregano
1 tablespoon garlic powder
1 teaspoon paprika
1 teaspoon cayenne pepper
1 tablespoon salt
1 teaspoon freshly ground pepper
CRISCO® Canola Oil* as needed for frying

*Or use your favorite CRISCO® Oil

In a shallow baking dish, whisk together the buttermilk and red pepper sauce. Add chicken pieces and turn to coat. Cover and refrigerate for a minimum of 2 hours and up to 24.

In a shallow baking dish, whisk together the PILLSBURY BEST® Flour, oregano, garlic powder, paprika, cayenne pepper, salt and freshly ground pepper. Toss the chicken pieces in the seasoned flour, a few at a time, until well coated. Dip chicken in the buttermilk mixture, then coat again in flour mixture.

In a large heavy skillet, pour CRISCO® Oil to a depth of 1 inch. Heat the oil to 350°F. (Use a deep fryer thermometer to measure the temperature.)

Carefully add chicken pieces in a single layer, skin side down. Fry about 4 minutes; turn over and fry the other side for about 4 minutes. Turn again, frying a total of about 15 minutes, or until chicken is evenly golden brown and crisp.

Carefully remove cooked chicken from pan. Place on a paper towel-lined plate to drain. Serve warm or at room temperature.   *Makes 4 servings*

Greek Chicken

1. Preheat oven to 375°F. Arrange garlic in shallow roasting pan. Place chicken pieces over garlic. Combine oil, 2 tablespoons lemon juice and rosemary in small bowl; brush evenly over chicken. Sprinkle chicken with salt and pepper. Bake 50 to 55 minutes or until juices run clear or internal temperature of thigh is 160°F. Transfer chicken to serving platter; keep warm.

2. Remove and discard skins from roasted garlic. Place garlic back in roasting pan; add remaining 2 tablespoons lemon juice. Cook over medium heat, mashing garlic and stirring to scrape up browned bits. Pour sauce over chicken; garnish with lemon peel and rosemary sprigs, if desired.

Makes 4 servings

Hint: Add more garlic and lemon juice to taste. Tuck a few lemon wedges or slices among the chicken pieces before roasting.

Tip: Unpeeled cloves of garlic usually burst open while roasting, making it a cinch to squeeze out the softened, creamy roasted garlic with your thumb and forefinger. If the cloves have not burst open, simply slice off the end with a knife and squeeze out the garlic.

12 large cloves garlic, unpeeled
3 pounds leg and thigh pieces or chicken quarters
3 tablespoons olive oil
4 tablespoons fresh lemon juice, divided
2 tablespoons chopped fresh rosemary *or* 2 teaspoons dried rosemary
¾ teaspoon salt
½ teaspoon black pepper
1 teaspoon finely shredded lemon peel
Additional sprigs fresh rosemary, lemon slices and roasted garlic cloves (optional)

Continental Chicken

1 package (2¼ ounces) dried beef, cut into pieces

4 boneless skinless chicken breasts (about 1 pound)

4 slices lean bacon

1 can (10¾ ounces) condensed cream of mushroom soup, undiluted

¼ cup all-purpose flour

¼ cup sour cream

Hot cooked noodles

Slow Cooker Directions

1. Spray inside of slow cooker with nonstick cooking spray. Place dried beef in bottom of slow cooker. Wrap each piece of chicken with one bacon slice. Place wrapped chicken on top of dried beef.

2. Combine soup, flour and sour cream in medium bowl; mix until smooth. Pour over chicken.

3. Cover; cook on LOW 7 to 9 hours or on HIGH 3 to 4 hours. Serve over noodles. *Makes 4 servings*

Serving Suggestion: Serve over hot buttered noodles.

Cream of Mushroom Soup

SOUR CREAM

Orange Pecan Chicken

In a medium bowl, whisk together juice and oil until well blended. Add salt and pepper to taste.

Place chicken breasts in plastic resealable food storage bag. Pour juice mixture over chicken; seal bag. Marinate in refrigerator 30 minutes. Meanwhile, prepare Orange Pecan Sauce.

Preheat broiler. Remove chicken from bag; discard marinade. Broil chicken about 6 or 8 minutes on each side or until no longer pink in the center, turning once. Serve chicken with Orange Pecan Sauce.

Makes 4 servings

1 cup orange juice
¼ cup vegetable oil
   Salt and black pepper to taste
4 boneless chicken breasts
   Orange Pecan Sauce (recipe follows)

Orange Pecan Sauce

Combine orange juice, butter, teriyaki sauce and garlic in small saucepan. Bring to a simmer over medium heat. Cook and stir 2 to 3 minutes or until well blended. Add brown sugar. Cook and stir 4 to 5 minutes or until combined and sauce is slightly thickened. Remove from heat. Stir in pecans and red pepper. Serve warm or at room temperature over chicken.

Makes about 1 cup

⅓ cup frozen orange juice concentrate, thawed
⅓ cup butter or margarine
2 tablespoons teriyaki sauce
1 clove garlic, minced
2 tablespoons packed dark brown sugar
2 tablespoons chopped toasted pecans
   Dash ground red pepper

Acknowledgments

The publisher would like to thank the companies and organizations listed below for the use of their recipes and photographs in this publication.

Allen Canning Company

Birds Eye Foods

Butterball® Turkey

Crisco is a registered trademark of The J.M. Smucker Company

Delmarva Poultry Industry, Inc.

Del Monte Corporation

Dole Food Company, Inc.

Grandma's® is a registered trademark of Mott's, LLP

Heinz North America

The Hidden Valley® Food Products Company

Holland House® is a registered trademark of Mott's, LLP

The Kingsford® Products Co.

Lawry's® Foods

McIlhenny Company (TABASCO® brand Pepper Sauce)

Ortega®, A Division of B&G Foods, Inc.

Pacific Northwest Canned Pear Service

Reckitt Benckiser Inc.

Riviana Foods Inc.

Unilever Foods North America

Veg•All®

Index

Metric Conversion Chart

VOLUME MEASUREMENTS (dry)

⅛ teaspoon = 0.5 mL
¼ teaspoon = 1 mL
½ teaspoon = 2 mL
¾ teaspoon = 4 mL
1 teaspoon = 5 mL
1 tablespoon = 15 mL
2 tablespoons = 30 mL
¼ cup = 60 mL
⅓ cup = 75 mL
½ cup = 125 mL
⅔ cup = 150 mL
¾ cup = 175 mL
1 cup = 250 mL
2 cups = 1 pint = 500 mL
3 cups = 750 mL
4 cups = 1 quart = 1 L

VOLUME MEASUREMENTS (fluid)

1 fluid ounce (2 tablespoons) = 30 mL
4 fluid ounces (½ cup) = 125 mL
8 fluid ounces (1 cup) = 250 mL
12 fluid ounces (1½ cups) = 375 mL
16 fluid ounces (2 cups) = 500 mL

WEIGHTS (mass)

½ ounce = 15 g
1 ounce = 30 g
3 ounces = 90 g
4 ounces = 120 g
8 ounces = 225 g
10 ounces = 285 g
12 ounces = 360 g
16 ounces = 1 pound = 450 g

DIMENSIONS

1/16 inch = 2 mm
⅛ inch = 3 mm
¼ inch = 6 mm
½ inch = 1.5 cm
¾ inch = 2 cm
1 inch = 2.5 cm

OVEN TEMPERATURES

250°F = 120°C
275°F = 140°C
300°F = 150°C
325°F = 160°C
350°F = 180°C
375°F = 190°C
400°F = 200°C
425°F = 220°C
450°F = 230°C

BAKING PAN SIZES

Utensil	Size in Inches/Quarts	Metric Volume	Size in Centimeters
Baking or Cake Pan (square or rectangular)	8×8×2	2 L	20×20×5
	9×9×2	2.5 L	23×23×5
	12×8×2	3 L	30×20×5
	13×9×2	3.5 L	33×23×5
Loaf Pan	8×4×3	1.5 L	20×10×7
	9×5×3	2 L	23×13×7
Round Layer Cake Pan	8×1½	1.2 L	20×4
	9×1½	1.5 L	23×4
Pie Plate	8×1¼	750 mL	20×3
	9×1¼	1 L	23×3
Baking Dish or Casserole	1 quart	1 L	—
	1½ quart	1.5 L	—
	2 quart	2 L	—